Spiritual Enlightenment - A Guide to Finding Spiritual Enlightenment

The Spiritual Keys to Awakening Your True Self Within Your False Self

Author: Piia Rauha

Free Gift

This book includes a bonus booklet. This giveaway may be for a limited time only. All information on how you can secure your gift right now can be found at the end of this book.

Table of Contents

Go from Stress to Success with These 15 Powerful Tips

You're in The Tunnel, Now Turn on The Light:

Here are The Best Ways to Transform Your Success

Do You Feel Stressed-Out, Overwhelmed and Harassed Every Day?

Then you're stuck in a negative thought spiral that is keeping you from achieving *real success!*

How many times have you thought, 'if only I could be more productive, then I'd get ahead?' No matter how hard you try, it eludes you. Most people experience intense self-doubt, worry and negative thinking at some point in their careers. These are your immediate obstacles to success.

This guide tackles these issues with easy, direct solutions to help you break the cycle and get back on track. These 15 powerful tips will take you from overwhelmed to overjoyed, in no time!

This FREE Cheat Sheet contains:

- Essential tips on how to stop worrying and start living

- How to actually relieve anxiety and banish it for good

- Ways to get rid of negative thoughts, and how to stop them from recurring

- Tips to become the most productive, motivated version of yourself

- How to focus on career success and build positive cycles and habits

Scroll down and click the link **below to Claim your Free Cheat Sheet!**

I want you to know that you don't have to live this way. You don't have to feel like these negative cycles are getting the better of you. Your career is waiting to bloom – and flourish! Give yourself the opportunity to make the right choices, by learning how to authentically reach for lasting success.

Ditch the stress, embrace success.

Click Here!

Book Description
Spiritual Enlightenment

Spiritual Enlightenment: The Spiritual Keys to Awakening Your True Self Within Your False Self explores how you can open the door to understanding who you truly are. By reading and heeding what this book recommends, you will begin the journey toward living a life full of bliss and spiritual enlightenment.

This guide covers a wide array of fascinating aspects about spiritual enlightenment and awakening, such as living consciously: the way out of pain, third eye awakening, who are you really? Are you your mind? And so much more. Some of the issues discussed in this guide reflect on the everyday challenges that we face in life. For instance, we all suffer the burden of living with pain without ever finding time to live happily. In addition, we are often blinded by our quest for material things.

It is by reading this book that you will understand that your quest for material things will only lead to temporary happiness. The reality of the matter is that true happiness comes from within. This happiness can only be attained by first knowing who you truly are.

People have spent decades looking for light in the darkness. It is time that you wake up from your sleep and realize that you are not your mind. Undeniably, the time to break away from your mind is now. Some exciting topics to look forward to in this manual include:

Piia Rauha

- You are not your mind

- Awakening and enlightenment explored

- Portals into the unmanifested

- Kill the Buddha

- Right here, right now!

- Feelings and emotions; understanding the difference

- And so much more!

Introduction

It is a ridiculous idea to think that there is anyone who can define what enlightenment is. In fact, this is one of the biggest problems about spiritual enlightenment. The mere fact that we have to use words fails to give us the actual understanding of what enlightenment is. When letters are put together to form words, it helps the mind to translate the information into something meaningful. However, it is worth noting that words will only have a meaning if you have experiential knowledge about what the words are trying to imply.

Let's say you are blind. This doesn't mean that you can understand color by only words. Similarly, music cannot be explained by using only words. The same case applies to love. Love cannot be explained to another person by using just words. Words are an effective means of communication only when someone understands what the words are trying to explain. Therefore, concerning enlightenment, this is not something that someone else has experienced. As a result, using words to define enlightenment might not convey the actual meaning of it.

Nevertheless, this will not limit us from crafting the best definition of spiritual enlightenment. Essentially, enlightenment refers to the discovery of your true, eternal self. It can also be defined as the complete dissolution of your identity as a separate being. In this case, it means separating yourself from your egoic mind. Right from birth, different people take on varying identities or roles that we perceive as real. However, what we fail to realize is that these identities that we assume are transitory and impermanent. Therefore, the labels are not our ultimate selves. Basing on this, spiritual enlightenment refers to the journey toward discovering our true selves.

Instead of identifying ourselves to things that are subject to change, spiritual awakening defines who we truly are. Anything that changes cannot be seen as a reality. When we find out who we truly are, we will live in the present moment without suffering. Spiritual awakening frees us from mental distress. Often, people find themselves suffering because they falsely identify themselves with things that change. We closely identify ourselves with our egoistic minds. Therefore, we end up living short of our expectations because we do not live in the here and now.

What we ought to realize is that our real self doesn't change; it's eternal. The discovery of the truth of who you really are is termed as spiritual awakening.

Most spiritual gurus agree that we are all spiritually enlightened. We all have the potential of being spiritually aware. The only difference is that not all people will realize that they are capable of being spiritually awake. Still, not just any realization can be identified as spiritual awakening. The point here is that your realization might be in the form of reading books, online articles, watching spiritual videos, etc. But this form of realization cannot be counted as spiritual awakening. As previously mentioned, love cannot be defined by just words. You have to experience love for you to understand what it truly means. The same case applies to spiritual enlightenment.

Enlightenment is not a concept to be understood. Instead, it is an experience to be lived. The experience of spiritual enlightenment varies from one person to the other. This experience is unique for every individual.

Another question that could be ringing in your mind is what could lead to spiritual enlightenment? Indeed, this is a complicated question to answer. Consider how flowers blossom. Have you ever stopped to ask yourself what made the flowers to blossom as they are? What were the factors that contributed to the blossoming of the flowers? The truth is that we cannot directly link the beautiful flowers we see to their origin. We only tend to appreciate how the flowers look. However, if you dig in deeper, you will realize that numerous things lead to the way the flowers look. Interestingly, all these factors had to work together toward giving the flowers their precious look.

Taking the above into consideration, spiritual enlightenment can be defined as the flowering of your consciousness. There is a huge mystery about how this happens. But, what you should understand is that it is an outcome contributed by several other outcomes. Accordingly, we cannot accurately pinpoint when the spiritual enlightenment flower will blossom.

Generally, it can be argued that spiritual awakening occurs when one finds their true self. It happens when an individual gains consciousness of their true nature. When all this is happening, there are cosmic forces that will work together to ensure that one is spiritually enlightened. For instance, through spiritual awakening, there are certain feelings that one will feel that they have never experienced before. One will notice that they are not connected with their physical bodies, but they are in harmony with the universe. What occurs here is that you are freed from your ego and you become more refined and attuned to your true self. The deeper you get into knowing your true self, the more your egoistic mind is silenced. The clutter in your mind that prevents you from thinking straight will be silenced. As a result, this opens doors to happiness. The interferences of worldly desires will be broken down by spiritual enlightenment.

This book will take you through an in-depth analysis of what spiritual enlightenment is. It will help you to understand some of the fundamental obstacles that prevent people from being spiritually enlightened. With the spiritual awakening knowledge that you will gain, you will begin accepting the reality of things as they are. The idea here is that you cannot control what's happening around you. Therefore, there is no need for you to be judgmental about it. Spiritual enlightenment will ensure that you experience life in ways that you never imagined before. You will start approaching life with an uncluttered mind that is not interrupted by worldly desires.

You might be in a dark place today, and the only remedy to this is illuminating some light in your dark world. Knowledge about spiritual enlightenment will bring this light to your world.

This book comes with a FREE Bonus chapter section as a gift. You can download them for free. The free content can be found at the bottom of this book.

Chapter 1
You Are Not Your Mind

"Our essential nature is one of pure potentiality"

– Deepak Chopra

Now you can describe what spiritual enlightenment is in words. It's the journey toward finding your true self. Just as a reminder, spiritual enlightenment is not a concept to be understood. Instead, it's an experience to be lived. Bearing this in mind, we have to stop and question ourselves why most people are not spiritually enlightened. It is by finding answers to this question that we can find a way toward awakening your inner self. This chapter looks into your mind being one of the greatest obstacles to enlightenment. This section will help you understand why your mind prevents you from being spiritually conscious and how you can free yourself from your mind. We'll also outline several pointers that can help you to rise above your thoughts.

Understanding The Greatest Obstacle to Enlightenment

Before getting into detail about spiritual enlightenment, it is evident that such spiritual awakening is a good thing. When you let go of your ego, there is no doubt that you will live a more fulfilling life. When you are enlightened, you will fill the void left by worldly desires with happiness. You will be filled with positivity and you will feel calmer. This is because your mind is free from clutter that prevents it from focusing on the present.

With these benefits of spiritual enlightenment, why is it that people find it daunting to be enlightened? What makes it so difficult to

Piia Rauha

be spiritually awake? Consider an ordinary example of a beggar sitting by the roadside. This beggar had been sitting in the same location for more than 30 years. At one point, a stranger walked passed him. The beggar did what he used to do and asked the stranger for some change. Well, the stranger had nothing to give and he made it clear to the beggar. However, instead of continuing with his journey, the stranger stopped for a moment and asked the beggar, "What are you sitting on?" Without hesitation, the beggar quickly replied, "Nothing, it's just an old box that I have been sitting on for years now." "Have you ever opened the box? asked the stranger. The beggar went ahead and explained to the stranger that there was no point of opening the box since there was nothing inside. Out of curiosity, the beggar decided to open the box. Alas! The box was full of gold.

What does this parable tell you? Have you ever stopped to look inside your box? Taking time to find your true self will unveil the real gold that lies deep inside you. The journey toward spiritual enlightenment will open your eyes to the realization that you are not who you have been thinking. All along, you have merely understood yourself by believing in the perceptions that your mind holds about you.

Identifying with your mind prevents you from realizing your very nature. This is because your mind is filled with compulsive thoughts. In this regard, you will find that you cannot stop thinking. Emotions and feelings have clouded your mind to the point that you cannot think straight. To most people out there, they call this "stress." Unfortunately, you don't realize quickly enough that you are suffering because everybody is complaining about how they can't stop thinking. As such, you also end up concluding that it's reasonable to overthink.

The constant mental noise deters you from connecting with your inner self. The worst thing is that your thoughts create a different you that believes in suffering. It fills you with anxiety about things that are yet to happen. What you don't realize is that anything that changes cannot define your true nature. You are far beyond that and to reach this realm of understanding, you need to free yourself from your mind.

Accordingly, the greatest obstacle to enlightenment is your mind. The world is filled with all sorts of problems that we cannot deny. This means that we are always bombarded with compulsive thoughts. Sadly, we fall into an empty hole where we identify ourselves with these thoughts. Our compulsive thinking separates us from our true nature. At one point in life, you might be thinking that everything is not working out as you had expected. Financially, you can seem to find a way out of your troubles. The first thing that comes to mind is that you're broke. For a while, this is what rings in your head most of the time. Well, the truth is that this is not you. It is just a phase in life. The best thing that you can do is to separate yourself from your thoughts. They are just thoughts and that's it.

Enlightenment can, therefore, be taken to mean the end of suffering and enslavement to your ceaseless thoughts. Without doubt, this is the highest form of liberation that you deserve to experience.

Associating with your mind blocks you from connecting with your inner self. It creates an opaque screen between you and God, between you and other human beings, between you and nature, between you and your inner self. So, your mind only blinds you from realizing that there is more to life than the concepts, words, judgments, definitions and the images that the blind has created about life. Eventually, you end up forgetting that beneath your understanding, there is you;

someone who cannot be defined by just physical appearances or by material things.

Maybe you do believe that it is true that you have forgotten who you truly are. However, just believing comforts you. But in the real sense, you can only liberate yourself by experiencing what it means to be enlightened.

Today, thinking has escalated into a disease. When you break down the term "di-sease," it means that your body is not at ease. Things are out of balance. This means that you are not yourself. The interesting thing about the mind is that it is a powerful tool that can transform your life if used in the right way. However, if not used properly, it is a destructive tool. Just to ensure that we are on the same page here, it is not that people don't use the mind rightly, they don't use it completely. Rather, it's the mind that uses them. This is what leads to the thinking disease that we are talking about. You reach a point where you become a prisoner to your mind. Basically, the mind has taken charge of you and you're no longer yourself.

The bitter truth about the mind is that there is no "off" button that you can press. This means that you cannot wake up one morning and choose to be free of your mind. So, you can only stop thinking for a while, but you can't shut down your mind completely. Therefore, in a way, your mind will use you. The mere fact that you unconsciously associate yourself with your mind implies that you are a slave to your mind. You might not realize this, but in reality, the mind is in control.

The first step toward spiritual enlightenment is realizing that you are not in control of your mind. The significance of this is that it helps you realize that you have the power of observing "the thinker"—your mind. Accordingly, when you start observing the thinker from a different standpoint, you awaken a higher level of consciousness. From this standpoint, you broaden your understanding beyond your thoughts. You will open doors to a higher level of intellect. In this case, your thoughts will only be a small fraction of your intellect. With this profound level of understanding, your eyes will be open to the realization that there are certain things in life that truly matter. Some of them include creativity, inner peace, beauty, love, and joy. Spiritually speaking, you will be enlightened, free from the captivity that your mind has placed you.

Freeing Yourself From Your Mind

Get it right; you are not your mind. You need to master how you can free yourself from your mind. Usually, we all have an inner voice that keeps talking to us. Have you ever heard this voice in your head? Maybe you have several voices speaking to you. The truth is that you have the power to control your inner voice. There is a good chance that you have come across a mad person walking down the street, talking to themselves. Funny enough, this is what we also do. The only difference is that a crazy person will do this aloud, but we tend to do it inside our minds.

Your inner voice can take any direction. It can like or dislike something, it can judge, complain, compare, and so on. The worst thing about this voice is that it is not always relevant to our present moments. Often, it takes us to our past, or that it flies us to our future. It will put you in a state of worry as you will ruminate about what can be instead of living in the present. Additionally, it will take you through a past that will only invite negative emotions your way. You will find yourself playing horrifying mental movies about your past or your present. The mental images created about your future might appear as good, but it only makes you worry. You will wonder whether you will indeed live the life that you are thinking about. This worry spurs anxiety and eventually robs you from being truly happy about your present life.

As you can see, your inner voice can be your worst enemy if not controlled or stopped. Many people have been tortured by their inner voices. They are never happy as their minds are full of these thoughts tormenting them. At the end of the day, they lack the energy they need to experience the beauty of life. This is one of the leading causes of depression.

Fortunately, you have the power to take charge of your mind and ensure that it doesn't use you. You can liberate yourself from your mind by listening to your inner voice. It is important to raise your awareness about what your mind is thinking about. Remember the notion of observing "the thinker" we talked about previously? Well, this is what you ought to be doing more often. Your mind has a mind of its own. You should observe it impartially. This is to mean that you shouldn't be judgmental about what your mind is thinking. Instead, your role is to listen to it and be aware. With time you will realize that "the thinker" is not you. It's just doing what it normally does; thinking.

Soon, you will be more conscious of the fact that there are thoughts running in your mind and these thoughts do not determine who you are. In other words, you will awaken a sense of constant presence in everything that goes on around you. This is your inner self. The true version of yourself that never changes regardless of what happens in this world. Ultimately, your thoughts will have no power over you. Compulsive thinking will gradually come to an end. At first, when compulsive thinking subsides, you will notice that there is silence in your mind. Well, this might last for a few seconds during the first few stages of your enlightenment, but rest assured that the silence will last longer in due course.

As your mind quiets down, you will realize that there is peace growing within you. Ideally, this is the onset of your true sense of "Being." Practice makes perfect. Therefore, if you practice more often to observe the thinker and quiet your mind, then you will reap the fruits of a deeper state of self-awareness. The most exciting feeling is that you will also enjoy the happiness that comes within you. This is the bliss of your Being.

Maybe you are thinking that the joy of Being will be a trance-like feeling. No! You will be more aware of yourself. Therefore, your happiness will not rob you of your consciousness. It's just a higher level of happiness that you might have never experienced before since it's coming from within you. From your state of pure consciousness, you will want to believe that there is nothing that can be compared to what you are feeling. As we had stated in the beginning, enlightenment cannot accurately be defined using words. It has to be experienced. So, there is no perfect way of describing how you will be feeling the moment you plant a seed of enlightenment inside you.

Besides listening to your thoughts and playing the role of an observer, meditation can also help you strengthen your self-awareness muscles. Meditating regularly will help you catch yourself overthinking. The exercises will drive you to develop a higher state of consciousness. Therefore, instead of your mind drifting into the past or future, meditation exercises will quieten it down and bring it to the present. Take note of the fact that meditation can be done anywhere. Whether you are walking or sitting, you can meditate by simply training your mind to focus more on the present.

Your mind can control you in ways that you never thought of. Unfortunately, the mere fact that everybody overthinks blinds us from realizing that we are not actually using our minds. Instead, we have become prisoners of our minds. In line with this, the most important step toward enlightenment is separating yourself from your mind. Every time you quiet your mind, your self-awareness muscles grow stronger. Don't be surprised when you find yourself smiling after catching a voice inside your head. At this point, you will be more aware of your thoughts and that you will comprehend that they don't define who you are.

Enlightenment: Rising Above Your Thoughts

The idea of separating yourself from your mind might appear confusing since thinking is crucial to our survival. However, it is imperative to understand that the mind has its specific functions. When its use is over, you should not use it for the wrong purpose. About 70% of what people think about is mostly negative.[1] This means most of our thoughts are harmful. If you observe your thoughts keenly, you will notice that you mind constantly drifts to think about bad things. Such compulsive thinking drives us to think that we cannot control our minds. We end up allowing the mind to take charge of

---

[1] "How Negative is Your "Mental Chatter"? | Psychology Today." 10 Oct. 2013, https://www.psychologytoday.com/us/blog/sapient-nature/201310/how-negative-is-your-mental-chatter. Accessed 17 Sep. 2019.

things. Sadly, this only leads to pain as we cannot live up to the expectations of the mind.

Sure, you might be addicted to thinking or overthinking. The main reason why this happens is because you have allowed yourself to believe that you will not live or exist without thinking. Therefore, you find yourself in a trap. A trap that you created for yourself. Your mind will reserve your past since this is what you believe in. At the same time, your mind will want to live in the future, creating a false sense of fulfillment that you will achieve more. In reality, this is not you. It is only your egoistic mind taking control of things and preventing you from living in the present.

Usually, you will find yourself saying; "In future, when this happens, I will be happy and contented." Your mind will be deceiving you from holding the true key to liberation—living in the present. The bitter truth is that you will never be truly happy if you associate yourself with your mind. You will only be enlightened when you finally realize that your mind has been an obstacle all this while. Therefore, it is vital that you rise above your thoughts.

Chapter 2
Living Consciously:
The Way Out of Pain

"If you aren't in the moment, you're either looking forward to uncertainty, or back to pain and regret"

- Jim Carey

Pain is part of life, right? Regardless of how much you try to avoid pain in your life, you will always feel pain at some point in your life. However, the pain that most people go through is simply unnecessary. People suffer because they allow the mind to run the show. Often, when you experience pain, your pain could be linked to the resistance you are trying to portray toward the reality. You should realize that whatever you resist, persists. This means that by trying to resist something, you will end up suffering since it will persist. Accordingly, the more you resist, the more pain you will suffer.

No More Pain in the Present

The mind is a rebellious tool. It has a mind of its own, and it will try to rebel efforts to try and control it.[2] Usually, you might notice that the mind will want to go against something that you are planning to do. For instance, if you have a to-do list that you should follow, the mind will resist attempts toward sticking on the to-do list until the end of the

---

[2] "A Psychiatrist on Why Your Mind 'Has a Mind of Its Own ...." 12 Dec. 2016, https://www.thecut.com/2016/12/a-psychiatrist-on-why-your-mind-has-a-mind-of-its-own.html. Accessed 17 Sep. 2019.

day. It will come up with some excuses that you could leave some tasks behind and work on them tomorrow. Unfortunately, this leads to procrastination. With time, it develops into a habit that affects the quality of your life.

The point here is that the mind will deny you the opportunity of living in the moment. The mind is like a time machine. It lives in the past and in the present. Picture a scenario where humans were absent from Earth. Would it be possible to speak of time in the same way human beings do? Certainly not! If a bird was asked, What time is it? Chances are that it would simply say that the time is now. Simply put, there is no other time apart from now in the world of plants and other animals.

If you are looking to avoid living in pain in your life, it is imperative that you embrace the idea that the only time you have is now. Living in the present moment frees you from the need to worry about your future. You will also overcome the burden of dealing with past events that you don't want to remember. Surrender to the present moment and enjoy life as it is. This is the most fulfilling experience.

It is worth noting that life will not always be rosy. Therefore, expect that there are certain times that the present moment will not be as pleasant as you expect. But the reality is that it is the way it is. You just need to accept how life unfolds itself and move on. The problem with resisting unpleasant moments only leads to pain. Your mind will label such moments negatively, and it will drain your energy since you will want to judge such events and relate them to your life. By stepping out of the field of resistance to these events, you will allow the present to be as it is. There is nothing much that you can do about it. So, it is best that you let things fall into place.

By not resisting what the present holds for you, you gift yourself with the advantage of being uninfluenced by external circumstances. As a result, whether things work out to your favor or not, you will be happy. In other words, you will find inner peace. Accordingly, surrendering to the present moment helps to free you from pain.

Dissolving Your Past Pain

One of the main benefits of living in the present is that it ensures that you are free from your past. You might have gone through a challenging period in your recent past. If you can tap into your power of living in the now, then there is a certainty that you will keep suffering from the pains of your past events. The worst thing is that the burden from your past will keep piling. With time, the burden might be too heavy for you to carry. When this happens, you will be depressed. The weight of your pain might have robbed you of the energy you need to live life with happiness. For that reason, you must dissolve your past pain.

Going through painful emotions is a normal thing. The problem that we humans have is that sometimes we hold on to these emotions for too long. This creates what is termed as emotional pain.[3] After holding on to emotional pain for too long, it matures to become painbody. This is an energy entity that will reside in you for years. Painbody exists in your body as active or in dormant form. When your painbody shifts its status from dormant to active, the voice of your

---

[3] "Pain Body - What It Is and How To Be Free — InnerPeaceNow ...." 2 Sep. 2016, https://www.innerpeacenow.com/inner-peace-blog/pain-body. Accessed 17 Sep. 2019.

body is amplified through your inner voice. If you are not conscious about living in the present, there is a likelihood that you will identify yourself with the painbody. When this happens, your mind will believe all the negative things that your inner voice is saying about you.

If you are somewhere on your own, the painbody will gain more energy by feeding on any negative thought that comes. Its activity will heighten. You will notice that you can't stop thinking negatively. Day and night, you will feel as though the world is crumbling on you. After the painbody stops being active and becomes dormant again, you will feel tired and empty.

Do you really deserve to go through such pain? You were born to live a happy life. As a result, you must live consciously by noting if there is any sign of sadness in your life. You never know, the slightest form of sadness might be stirring up painbody inside you. Watch out for signs of impatience, depression, anger, irritability, and so on. Catch these feelings before it awakens the monster that has been living in you.

The Origin of Fear

The pain that you might be suffering from could be as a result of your underlying fear. Fear leads to emotional pain. With regard to this, you may have stopped and wondered how fear arises. What is its origin? Why is it that there are so many people living in fear? And isn't fear helpful at times, more so when it reminds you to protect yourself?

Well, to start with the issue of fire, the reason why you will stay away from a burning fire is that you are sure that you will get burned. So, fear will not help you steer away from unnecessary danger. Instead, intelligence will. Psychological fear that we are trying to talk about in this case is different from the fear of imminent danger you might face.

Psychological fear could be in the form of worry, tension, nervousness, anxiety, phobia, dread, uneasiness, etc. Clearly, psychological fear occurs out of something that could happen. It doesn't relate to anything happening now.

What this means is that you are in the present, but your mind is ruminating about the future. Anxiety is the resultant effect of living in the future. Accordingly, if you allow your mind to take control of things, there is a certainty that it will be daunting for you to cope with the present.

From afar, it might appear as though there are many causes of fear. Nevertheless, fear is associated with an egoic mind. This is a mind that is always feeling that they are under threat. Such a mind will even fear the fact that they might lose an argument. It is essential to realize that there is no power in being perceived as better than others. The real power is within you. Therefore, you must disidentify yourself from your mind. This is because the mind can blind you to believe in what can be changed. Ideally, this is not the real you. Your true self lies within and it's up to you to connect with it.

The Ego's Search for Wholeness

Have you ever felt that you are not worthy enough in life? If this is a feeling that you have felt at one point in your life, then it is your egoic mind trying to search for wholeness. An egoic mind will have the feeling that it is incomplete and, therefore, will do anything to fill the void inside you. People can experience this emptiness either consciously or unconsciously. If you are experiencing this consciously, you will feel as though you are not good enough in front of other people. On the other hand, if you experience this unconsciously, then you feel as though you need something in your life to complete you.

In both cases, people will often seek ways of feeding their egos. For instance, it is not uncommon to find individuals searching for material wealth with the hope that it will make them happy. Others will yearn to associate with a certain group of friends so that they can fit into a particular social status. Unfortunately, even after achieving these things, people end up realizing that they are still empty. In fact, it is as this point they realize that things are even worse than before. This is because they will be more disappointed with their efforts in striving to achieve that which consumed a lot of their time.

When an egoic mind is running the show, you will never be at peace with yourself. You will only be happy for a moment when your desires are fulfilled. But you should bear in mind that this is brief since your egoic mind will desire for something else after achieving what you wanted earlier on. An important thing worth mentioning is that the ego is a derived perception that is not you. Accordingly, it tends to relate itself to external things. This is the main reason why your ego will need to be fed constantly. People who allow their ego to get the best of them will identify themselves with material possessions, social status, special abilities, family history, physical appearance, and other shared identifications. The reality is that this is not you.

Maybe you are finding this frightening because you just realized that all you have been chasing all along will not lead to happiness as you had thought. But, it is important that you understand this now rather than later. It might be hard to believe that you cannot find true happiness from external things. True happiness lies within you. Later on, when death approaches, you will realize that all these external things prevented you from meeting with your true self. The secret here is that it is better if you die before you die.[4] What this means is that death of identifying yourself with your mind should happen now as this will liberate you to true happiness.

---

[4] "How To Die Before You Die - Monty Winters." 28 Jul. 2013, http://montywinters.com/awareness/die-before-you-die/. Accessed 18 Sep. 2019.

Chapter 3
Third Eye Awakening

"It is through gratitude for the present moment that the spiritual dimension of life opens up"

- Eckhart Tolle

In simple terms, the third eye is often referred to as the "eye of knowledge."[5] We all have five senses. Awakening the third eye refers to the process of awakening your sixth sense. When you open your third eye, you will have a higher sense of wisdom and intuition. The main reason why spiritual gurus refer to the sixth sense as the third eye is because it's the mind's eye positioned between your eyebrows. Usually, the third eye chakra is awakened when an individual reaches a high level of consciousness and awareness. This section goes forth to discuss more about the third eye and ways in which you can achieve a high level of self-awareness and consciousness as recommended.

Understanding the Third Eye

If you have never heard the term "third eye" before, then you must be wondering what this is. Simply put, this is the gate that opens you to a realm of a higher level of consciousness and your inner world. This eye is located in the pineal gland, between your eyebrows.[6] Everybody has a

---

[5] "Third Eye Awakening Explained - Inner Outer Peace." https://innerouterpeace.com/third-eye-awakening/. Accessed 18 Sep. 2019.

[6] "Third Eye Guide - A Personal Tao." https://personaltao.com/third-eye/. Accessed 18 Sep. 2019.

third eye. The only problem is that developing the third eye chakra is challenging. To most people, this is a feat that seems out of reach. Nevertheless, this book will reveal to you a few secrets that you can utilize to awaken your third eye.

The presence of the third eye could be perceived as a 'switch.' It is a switch that can activate a more profound sense of self-consciousness. Individuals who can better connect with their third eye open their bodies to higher energy frequencies. As a result, they can see things clearer and deal with their problems effectively. In this case, both emotional and physical disorders can be treated with the third eye. The healing power of the third eye stems from the fact that people are more connected with their true selves. However, this doesn't mean that third eye awakening will heal everything in your body. The point is that there is a greater potential in the healing power of the third eye.

Spiritually, most people will seek to open their third eye with the intention of seeking spiritual fulfillment. This because the third eye gives you a chance to connect with your true self. You see things clearly with an open mind. The intellectual balance gained from third eye awakening also makes individuals seek the purest form of happiness that is not found in external things.

Awakening Your Third Eye

So, how do you awaken your third eye? Of course, this is one of the main questions that you have in mind regarding the third eye. The first thing that you should understand about third eye awakening is that it is not easy. Well, this shouldn't scare you. The point here is that you should be patient enough for this to happen. It is not something that you can achieve overnight. Nevertheless, with practice, you will open yourself to a realm of higher levels of intuition, self-awareness and consciousness. The following is a succinct look at how the third eye can be awakened.

Using Meditation

Meditation is something that has hit the headlines over the past few years. The popularity of meditation has been influenced by its mental and physical benefits to the body. Essentially, meditation is when you allow things to be as they are. It is when you stop judging things around you, but you just let them be as they are.[7]

Before getting into detail about meditation, an important step that you should take is to locate your third eye chakra. Chakras is a term referring to your body's energy centers. We all have seven chakras including:

1. Root chakra

2. Sacral chakra

3. Solar plexus chakra

4. Heart chakra

5. Throat chakra

6. Third eye chakra

7. Crown chakra

---

[7] "Third Eye Awakening Explained - Inner Outer Peace."
https://innerouterpeace.com/third-eye-awakening/. Accessed 18 Sep. 2019.

When thinking about these chakras, consider them as ideal pathways that ensure your body, mind and soul are in harmony.[8] As indicated above, third eye chakra is the sixth on the list. During meditation, your focus will be placed on this chakra.

For you to meditate effectively, one of the most important things that you should do is to find a comfortable place to sit. The environment you choose will determine whether or not you will be able to find the focus you are looking for. Another crucial aspect of meditation is the posture that you take. The body and the mind should be connected without being interrupted by pain resulting from a bad sitting posture. It is for this reason that you should find a relaxed body position that doesn't strain your body.

The other thing you should focus on is finding a meditation object. This is your object of focus. It can be something physical or just a thought that can put your mind to focus. Usually, when awakening the third eye, your object of focus will be the point between your eyebrows (the third eye). Your concentration will be directed to this area as everything else that flows in your mind will be brought to your awareness. Before using the third eye as your object of focus, you might want to start with other physical objects such as candles. At first, this will make it easier for you to concentrate since you will be focusing on something that you can actually see.

---

[8] "The 7 Chakras For Beginners ...." 10 Sep. 2019, https://www.mindbodygreen.com/0-91/The-7-Chakras-for-Beginners.html. Accessed 18 Sep. 2019.

In addition to the above, you will also require a mantra. This is a word or phrase that you constantly repeat while meditating.[9] An ideal mantra should be something that resonates with you. For instance, you can choose the word "peace" or the phrase "I choose happiness" as your mantra.

Meditation requires constant practice. This is not something that you do for a few weeks and forget about it. You have to develop a routine. You have to train your mind to meditate at a particular time every day. Practicing regularly ensures that you can turn it into a habit.

Practicing Mindfulness

Besides meditation, mindfulness can also be used to awaken your third eye. Living mindfully requires that you live consciously of the world around you. This means that you should be aware of anything and everything that happens around you. Simply put, it's practicing to live with a higher state of self-awareness about what is going on around you. Living with mindfulness is beneficial both emotionally and mentally. This is for the reasons that you will be more attuned to your thoughts and emotions. As a result, you can easily catch yourself when your mind is deviating from the present moment.

Mindfulness can be practiced in your everyday life. The idea is to be fully observant. For instance, if you have gone out to have fun with family and friends, you need to ensure that your mind is in the present moment with your loved ones. Of course, your mind will want to steer

_____

[9] "How To Open Your Third Eye: Awaken Your Spirituality." https://www.psychics4today.com/how-to-open-your-third-eye-chakra/. Accessed 18 Sep. 2019.

away from these moments. You might find yourself thinking about the pending project that is late or the worry that you may have forgotten to lock your door. It is important that you notice these thoughts coming and going inside your mind. With your sense of self-awareness, you can stop these thoughts and emotions. This is what living mindfully is all about.

Nurturing Your Creativity

Another practical way of awakening your third eye is by tapping into your creativity. Creativity allows your mind to wander freely on activities without being judgmental. Therefore, it doesn't matter whether you are doing something correctly or wrongly. The point is that you're honing your creative skills. Thus, nurturing your creativity loosens your rational mind. It quiets the mind, and you won't judge whether what you are doing is right or wrong. As a result, your egoic mind that desires to be in charge will not take control of things here. The effect of this is that it will open you to a world full of possibilities.

Benefits of Third Eye Awakening

There are numerous benefits of third eye awakening. Some of these benefits are briefly discussed.

Feel Peaceful

With third eye awakening, you will be more at peace with yourself. Your mind will rarely be in control of you. This is because of your heightened state of consciousness. The fact that you will be aware of what is going on inside your mind and in your external world means that you will find peace within yourself. Ultimately, this will help you fall in love with your true self.

More Intelligent

You cannot overlook the fact that your third eye will help you see things from a different perspective. You will often avoid the idea of judging what is happening around you. You have a higher level of understanding that everything happens for a reason. What's more, you appreciate the importance of living in the present. As such, such intellect will ascertain that you relate with the world around you in the most profound ways.

A Healthier Body and Mind

Generally, you will also be a healthier individual emotionally, mentally and physically. Your higher levels of self-awareness will help you reduce stress. Instead of ruminating about the past and worrying about your future, third eye awakening will help you stay in the present and enjoy what you have now. By living in the here and now, there is a high likelihood that you will experience a wide array of health benefits.

Trusting Your Intuition

Still, on third eye awakening, it is worth noting that the sixth chakra can help you trust your intuition. This can lead you to make important life decisions, such as choosing the right spiritual path to follow. Usually, there are times when our bodies provide us with certain clues about the world around us. For instance, there are times when the body might tell you that something isn't right about what you are about to eat or drink. After consulting with a few people, you find out that your food or drink is okay. Later on, your stomach is affected and you realize that your intuition was right.

In the business world, at times, you might have a gut feeling that the business deal that you are about to enter into is not good. However, you choose to ignore your intuition hoping that things work out fine. Unfortunately, you later regret when the business deal turns sour. Such clues usually come and go and it is surprising to learn that your sixth chakra (the third eye) can help you in following your intuition.

How is this possible? Well, third eye awakening increases your self-awareness. You will learn to make better decisions. Your increased intellect will gift you with the power to discern between what is right and wrong. At times, you will be forced to make certain decisions because you strongly believe that it is the right thing to do. The best part is that you won't regret any decisions that you will make. This is because you would have asked your inner self for guidance on the best path to take. Your egoic mind might mislead you because there is a good chance that it will yearn to make you look worthy in front of others. Nevertheless, your inner chakra will help you connect with your inner self and determine the best decision to make.

Third eye awakening is an integral part of spiritual enlightenment. Earlier on, we had argued that spiritual enlightenment is an experience to be lived. Putting into words, it refers to the journey of finding your true self. Finding your inner self requires that you should obtain a higher level of consciousness. In this regard, you ought to be aware of the fact that your mind is not you. You should be more aware of the fact that your mind should not control you. This is where third eye awakening comes in. Through meditation and practicing mindfulness, you can open your third eye and become more aware about yourself and the world around you.

A Short message from the Author:

Hey, are you enjoying the book? I'd love to hear your thoughts!

Many readers do not know how hard reviews are to come by, and how much they help an author.

Customer Reviews

☆☆☆☆☆ 2
5.0 out of 5 stars ▾

5 star		100%
4 star		0%
3 star		0%
2 star		0%
1 star		0%

See all verified purchase reviews ›

Share your thoughts with other customers

Write a customer review

I would be incredibly grateful if you could take just 60 seconds to write a brief review on Amazon, even if it's just a few sentences!

>> Click here to leave a quick review

https://www.amazon.com/review/create-review?asin=B0817TB7MQ

Thank you for taking the time to share your thoughts!

Your review will genuinely make a difference for me and help gain exposure for my work.

Chapter 4
Awakening and
Enlightenment Explored

"If I could define enlightenment briefly I would say it is "the quiet acceptance of what is."

- Wayne Dyer

When we are asked about our spirituality, the first thing that comes to mind is whether we are religious or not. In line with this, it should be noted that spirituality doesn't necessarily relate to your religion. Thinking of spirituality in the context of religion only makes it confusing to understand what spirituality means. The term spiritual can, therefore, be defined as an attribute of being beyond the material or physical domain of existence.[10] Just like spirituality, enlightenment can mean several things. Nevertheless, it is often linked to matters relating to cognition.

What is Spiritual Awakening?

Spiritual awakening refers to the kindling of a dimension where one realizes that their egos do not confine them. In this regard, your ego is your sense of oneness, your exclusive notion of your being the "I."[11] Spiritual awakening occurs when an individual realizes that there is an

---

[10] "Spiritual Awakening Signs: 10 Authentic Symptoms + 5 ...." https://scottjeffrey.com/spiritual-awakening-signs/. Accessed 18 Sep. 2019.

[11] "Spiritual Awakening Signs: 10 Authentic Symptoms + 5 Spiritual Traps."

inner person that is beyond themselves. When your inner self arises above you, then you can say that you have spiritually awakened.

It can also be argued that spiritual awakening is where one's sense of consciousness arises to the extent where you open up to your true self. There are plenty of ways of describing spiritual awakening. It can also mean the flowering of your consciousness just as we had explained at the beginning of this book.

When you become more conscious about who you are, you see the world from a different angle. You will be more in control of your life and that you will make informed decisions leading to a happy and blissful life. Interestingly, you will connect more with your mind, body, and soul. The most exciting aspect of spiritual awakening is that you will notice a gradual shift in your energy levels. Your emotional, physical, and mental energy will be on a new level. In other words, you will be operating in frequencies that you have never known before. This is the new you.

How Does Spiritual Awakening Feel?

Words cannot accurately describe what spiritual awakening means. However, by talking about the experience of a spiritually awake individual, you will get a clear picture of what it means to be spiritually awake. The awakening process is slow and gradual. It is something that you begin to notice as life unfolds itself. People will differ in how they get spiritually awaken. When your eyes are opened to the realization that there is a higher self beyond what you understand, your ego surrenders to the spirit. In the world of Taoism, your lower soul refines itself into the higher soul.[12]

Spiritually-awake people will live their lives in a somewhat unique manner. These people will understand on a deeper level that they are renewed. They will perceive their lives like a play and that they are the actors on stage. What they comprehend is that they have a role to play in the act. Interestingly, regardless of how the act might appear to be difficult, they know that it's all but an act. This perception of their lives is quite liberating as it allows them to enjoy life, living each day without regret.

The best part is that spiritually-awake people also know that they are here to learn new things about their lives. Therefore, they acknowledge the fact that they are not perfect. If they fail in something today, tomorrow is another day to learn something new.

Following the deeper insight that spiritually awakened people have, they never bother themselves with things that they can't control. They pay little attention to negative things that could only drain energy from them. Since they focus their energy in living in the present, spiritually awakened people have a lot of energy to go through their every day with lots of passion.

Traits of Spiritual Awakening

To ensure that you understand how one can be spiritually awakened, it is vital to take a look at some of the characteristics which are evident in

---

[12] "Spiritual Awakening Signs: 10 Authentic Symptoms + 5 ...."
https://scottjeffrey.com/spiritual-awakening-signs/. Accessed 18 Sep. 2019.

such people. Before looking at the authentic signs of spiritual awakening, common misleading signs that you should watch out for include:

- Thinking you are better than others.

- Considering yourself as a spiritual being.

- Acting nice—a sign of psychological immaturity

- Thinking that others are evil

The experiences that people face differ as spiritual awakening is a personal experience. Nevertheless, common authentic characteristics are as briefly detailed.

Disidentifying Yourself from Your Mind

Often, a spiritually awake person will disidentify themselves from their mind. Instead of doing something because it is the right thing to do, they will do it because they love doing what they do. When they choose to love, they will love others because it is a feeling that comes from within. In other words, they will live through their hearts instead of their minds.

Peaceful Mind

Spiritually awake individuals will declutter their minds. They will get rid of the noise that often leads people to overthink and stress over issues that are beyond their control. An uncluttered mind leads to more clarity. One can reason more clearly than ever before. They see their lives from a different and elevated perspective. In addition, they are more conscious and aware of their thoughts. Accordingly, they live peaceful lives with minimal distractions from the external world.

Shift in Priorities and Values

Once you identify a higher authority within yourself, your priorities and values will change. For instance, religious people believe in acting morally based on a certain set of codes and standards. With spiritual enlightenment, individuals act based on a personal ethical framework. Here, they determine the best action to take at a particular moment. It is for this reason that spiritually awake people will portray noticeable behavioral changes.

Change in Lifestyle Choices

There will also be a massive change in your lifestyle choices once you become spiritually awake. The normal things that you once did before will become unacceptable. Your higher level of consciousness will enhance the connection you have with the environment. You will be more concerned about the environment. Ethically, you will want to live your life based on ideal moral standards.

Enhanced Intuition

Spiritually awakening also strengthens your intuition. You will be more aware of your sixth sense and will often follow your gut when making important life decisions. In most cases, you will want to believe that your higher self is talking to you. As a result, this creates a scenario where you think less over certain things. With your inner-self taking charge, you will be able to look at things clearer than before.

Your inner knowing will also be enhanced by a huge margin. There are numerous things that you will be aware of without thinking logically about them. For example, you won't have to waste time differentiating between what is right and wrong. You simply know the right path to take. Ideally, this makes your life easy and worth cherishing.

More Control of Your Life

Usually, people live their lives as though they were sailing through a stormy sea. They get tossed here and there. The challenges that they have to go through make their lives less interesting. All they see in life is a struggle. Nothing comes easy. Do you feel that your life is nothing but a struggle? If so, spiritual awakening will change that. Becoming awakened gives you the opportunity to control your life.

Spiritual awakening gives you a more in-depth insight into how you can live your life by creating your own world. For instance, it makes you understand how you can deal with negative thoughts and emotions. Therefore, by not surrounding yourself with negativity, there is a good chance that you will live a life full of optimism.

Spiritual Awakening and Enlightenment: The Difference

To this point, there is a good chance that you might be thinking that spiritual awakening and enlightenment are the same. The truth is that spiritual awakening and enlightenment are different. However, the two terms refer to a dramatic shift in your life. When you wake up in the morning, we usually refer to this process as awakening. You are waking up from your sleep. When waking up from slumberland, you wake up to connect with the real you.

Whenever you are sleeping, you are in a different world. Basically, you are dreaming of all the things that you can and cannot be.

Suddenly, when you wake up, you realize that you haven't moved an inch. You are in the same location you were a few hours before you went to bed. Now, after waking up, you realize that you need to go to work, school or attend to your daily routines. Ideally, this is the awakening experience that we go through on a regular basis.

Spiritually speaking, the life you are living now is like a dream. You are in a deep sleep. The person you think you are is not the real you. Awakening from this sleep, therefore, brings you to reality. It brings out the real you from within. Once you awaken, you realize that there is a different and enjoyable life worth living. You are happier and that life is more fulfilling than ever before.

Simply put, spiritual awakening refers to that very instance when you stop living your life in an auto-pilot mode. When you are awake, you will live a life with a sense of direction and purpose. Life will have a deeper meaning to you as you try to find yourself within it. However, you should note that you are not enlightened yet.

Sure, you are now awake, but you are not enlightened. All along, you might have been dealing with pain in your life. You have always been a prisoner of your mind. All this time, you have never enjoyed life because you don't understand the true meaning of living. So, this means that you need time to heal. Certainly, you cannot heal immediately after awakening. Once you are spiritually awake, you will take on another journey where you improve and continue discovering yourself. Accordingly, spiritual awakening is only the beginning of your journey to enlightenment.[13]

Enlightenment, therefore, means something of higher significance than awakening. It is a journey that you take toward finding your true self. After you are spiritually awake, you proceed with a long journey toward self-discovery, which is becoming enlightened. The reality about awakening is that you are either awake or asleep. You either know that there is a higher self inside you or not. On the contrary, enlightenment is not a two-way thing. It is a continuous process of self-discovery.

What Is It Like to Be Enlightened?

You might be wondering how it feels like to be enlightened. Well, enlightenment is a higher state of spiritual awakening and that it is an ongoing process. This means that you can't accurately pinpoint how one feels when they are enlightened. Some individuals will want to argue that being enlightened is being spiritually awake many times. However, this is a vague description as it doesn't really tell how one feels after being spiritually enlightened.

Enlightened people have a higher sense of peace, joy, and happiness in their lives. They also have an elevated sense of knowing. They don't have to think about things that much because they know. These people are also in harmony with the universe. Usually, they

––––––––––––––––––––––––

[13] "Spiritual Awakening is not the Same as Enlightenment - Heartki." 10 Nov. 2013, https://www.heartki.com/spiritual-awakening-enlightenment/. Accessed 19 Sep. 2019.

believe in loving unconditionally. This doesn't mean that they are perfect because sometimes they feel sad too.

Spiritually enlightened individuals also live in the present. They express the love they have for themselves and the world around them from within. The past is the past for them and the future is not for them to worry about. They relate to other people in admirable ways. The best part is that they feel their presence on earth in profound ways.

Rising Kundalini

Rising kundalini tells how we can notice when we are approaching enlightenment. Kundalini energy refers to a feminine energy that resides in each one of us.[14] This energy is often seen as a snake coiled up at the base of our spine or inside our belly. Of course, not all people will envision kundalini as a snake, but this is the common symbol used for kundalini energy.

Concerning kundalini awakening, this occurs when the snake inside you rises from the bottom of your belly or spine to the top of your head. This rising bears a huge impact on you since it awakens divine intelligence inside you. It connects the mind, heart, and the brain, restoring the divine energy that was lying within you.[15] When you experience kundalini awakening, this could be a clear sign that you are being enlightened.

---

[14] "What is a Kundalini Awakening? - Forever Conscious." https://foreverconscious.com/what-is-a-kundalini-awakening. Accessed 19 Sep. 2019.

[15] "What is a Kundalini Awakening? - Forever Conscious." https://foreverconscious.com/what-is-a-kundalini-awakening. Accessed 19 Sep. 2019.

Kundalini awakening is also a form of purification that one goes through. The rising of this energy from the bottom of your spine to your head cleanses you. It clears all the blockages that are usually brought about by emotional and mental baggage or the negativity that we have about life. Once kundalini energy flows in you, there is a deeper sense of positivity about life that awakens in you.

In a word, following what has been discussed about awakening and enlightenment, you now have a clear understanding that the two terms differ. In this case, you might be spiritually awakened, but you are not enlightened. Awakening is the beginning of your journey to finding your true nature. Enlightenment is the ongoing experience that you face toward reaching your highest level of consciousness. Therefore, there is no clear way of defining how it feels to be enlightened. What's more, different people have varying experiences concerning their enlightenment. All in all, awakening and enlightenment leads to a complete transformation of the person that you once were.

Chapter 5
Who Are You Really?
Are You Your Mind

"You have power over your mind—not outside events. Realize this, and you will find strength."

—*Marcus Aurelius*

An essential step in spiritual awakening and enlightenment is that you first have to find the inner you. As a result, this chapter will help you understand the inner you by first disidentifying yourself from your mind. We'll start with a brief meditation exercise to help you determine who you really are.

Find a quiet and comfortable place where you can meditate peacefully without interruptions. Sit down, relax and focus on your breathing. Take a deep breathe in while closing your eyes and breathe out. Take another deep breath, this time allowing your breath to suck up all the pressure and tension that lies within you. Breath out slowly, letting go of all the pressure and stress that was preventing your mind and body from relaxing.

Now you are in a relaxed state. As you continue breathing in and out, listen to your mind. Deep inside, thoughts and emotions are coming and going. Recognize the activity going on in your mind. Take note of these thoughts and emotions without doing anything about them. They are just thoughts and feelings. Notice how these feelings and thoughts are affecting how you feel.

From the observer's point that you have taken, watch your body from above. Where are you sitting? Can you notice the way you are seated from above? Can you see the position you have assumed while practicing this meditation?

Gradually, move inside you with the same perspective. How are you feeling now? Are you happy, sad, or confused? Maybe you are feeling tensed. Now shift your attention to your thoughts. What are you thinking about? Are these thoughts flowing freely or that you are thinking about certain things influencing them?

Gently bring your focus back to how you are breathing. Breathe in and out as you bring your mind back to reality. Open your eyes.

At first, meditation exercises might prove to be complicated. Often, this happens because you will find it challenging to maintain focus and observe your thoughts and feelings. You must practice meditation to strengthen your awareness muscles.

Following the short meditation exercise, an important question that you should ask yourself is who was observing your mind? Is it you that was observing the mind? Or was it your mind observing itself? Sounds confusing, right? Well, the point here is that you might have noticed that there was a different mind with a higher authority and awareness doing the observation. Interestingly, when you choose to live mindfully, you will always allow the higher mind to control things.

When your higher mind is running the show, it means that you are in close proximity to the real you. This is the inner you. The inner you is always unshaken by worry and fear. It never judges, but it understands life better. Moreover, it is always peaceful and joyful. The inner you has an identity that is not dependent on the past or the future. It is an unchanged version of yourself regardless of what happens. Whether you become rich, poor, famous or infamous, the inner you never changes. You should comprehend that the perceived change that you often go through as a result of external changes is your egoic mind pushing you to believe that you have changed. The reality is that your true self never changes.

From what we have said, you can conclude that there is a higher version of ourselves beyond what we think. But, how can we connect with our inner self?

Becoming the Inner You

The path toward enlightenment requires that you connect with the inner you and live in the same way that it lives. Fortunately, with regular meditation exercises, this can be achieved. The more you take the observer's role, watching how thoughts and emotions are flowing inside your mind, the more you connect with your inner self. The idea here is that you should enhance your consciousness. You must awaken your conscious self to direct you on how you should live your life.

The good news about spiritual awakening and enlightenment is that once you open your eyes to the realization that there is a higher self inside you, the intellect doesn't shrink the following day. Instead, your consciousness will continue to expand since you will be practicing meditation and mindfulness exercises on a regular basis. At times you will shift to use your analytical mind. This is a common thing that happens. However, this doesn't mean that you will forget about the presence of your higher self. The choice is yours on the kind of life that you want to live. Therefore, interest in becoming the inner you will determine how far you go with your journey toward enlightenment.

One thing that should be made clear is that the inner you is not some form of a person living inside you. Definitely not! Consequently, finding the inner you might prove to be difficult if you don't focus your attention on revealing your true self. Spiritual gurus, however, argue that the heart is the bridge or compass to finding the inner you.[16] As a result, living through your heart will naturally open your doors to your true nature. Maybe this is the main reason why most people will advise you to follow your heart when at crossroads. Usually, you are never told to follow your mind. Food for thought!

Connecting with Your Inner Higher Self

In the midst of trying to understand how to connect with your inner self, one question lingers; how far is your inner self? To answer this question, you should remember that your inner self is not an individual residing in you. When clearing the way to connect with your inner self, you should eliminate all the things that prevent you from reality. Indeed, it will take time to get rid of all the junk in your mind. Over the years, you have accumulated things that deter you from connecting with your true self. As a result, the first step toward connecting with your inner person is to make space.

Have you ever felt how peaceful it is to walk by the lake when no one is around? Or taking a walk somewhere in a hilly place with lots of trees? The light breeze away from town light often calms your mind. It washes away the thoughts that have been filling your mind all day. After taking on such walks, you usually feel lighter and energetic.

---

[16] "Finding Your Inner Compass - Kate De Jong." 4 Mar. 2017, https://katiedejong.com/finding-your-inner-compass/. Accessed 19 Sep. 2019.

Therefore, clearing your mind requires that you should empty all the conceptions that you have accumulated all this time. Dump all the ideas that you have about life, and you will feel your heart and soul getting lighter and lighter. The core of your inner being will begin to show. You will see and think more clearly. This is your awakening. Do this more often and practice meditation exercises and your footpaths toward enlightenment will start to show.

The best way of clearing the path toward finding the real you is to take on the role of the great observer.[17] As previously mentioned, you should assume the role of an observer each time you are thinking. This means taking a different angle toward what you are doing. In a way, you evaluate your thoughts and emotions. The advantage of doing this more often is that you will understand yourself better. Gradually, you will recognize your strengths and weaknesses. You will be in a better position to recognize your behaviors. With time, this brings you a sense of control in what you do about your life.

Another strategy that you can use is the idea of using other people to tell you about yourself. The people you choose for this exercise should be individuals that you trust that they can be honest with you. The vital thing to do here is that you should listen to what other people are saying without criticizing them or defending yourself. After having vital information about your beliefs, attitudes, opinions, behaviors and thoughts, you then decide how to eliminate all the negatives. Ideally, this is how you clear the way. The exciting thing is that you will be in

---

[17] "The Long Journey to the Inner Self | HuffPost Life." 23 Jun. 2014, https://www.huffpost.com/entry/the-long-journey-to-the-inner-self_b_5518540. Accessed 19 Sep. 2019.

better control of yourself. In other words, you will be changing the course of your ship (life). Since you are steering your ship, you will change its direction and move toward brighter skies. This is finding your true self.

Love for Self

With a clear understanding of how to clear the way toward finding your true self, what is holding you back from changing the course of your ship? Why are you waiting for a disaster to occur to make a move? The beauty of life is that we all have a choice to make. You can decide today to steer your ship and discover the true meaning of life.

Have you ever wondered how a child assumes everything around them and lives a life without worry, guilt, fear, and that they never judge? Undeniably, your inner self is like a child. Sure, there are times when a child gets sad, but this is wiped away with a smile on their face. It is crucial that you fall in love with the child within you. Unfortunately, we often ignore the importance of falling in love with our true selves. As we grow old, we tend to take life seriously. Work pressures and other responsibilities occupy most of our time. This prevents us from connecting with our inner person. From time to time, we allow our minds to drive us out of these pressures.

So, what do we do? We focus on money instead of happiness. We pay too much attention to material things hoping that they will satisfy our desires. Funny enough, some end up disliking their bodies. They end up allowing societal perceptions about body images to drive them. Honestly, this is not you. When you allow such perceptions to take over your life, it means that you are far away from the real you. Later, when we achieve what we yearned to acquire in life, we realize that the external world cannot make us happy.

The bitter consequence of allowing your egoic mind to run your life is that you will dislike yourself. You won't have any respect for your body. Health will not be as important to you. Chances are that you will not create time to enjoy life since you always think that money is the root of all happiness. The truth is that money is not a bridge to happiness. Spiritually speaking, true happiness comes from within. So, plant a seed of love within you as you show this love to yourself and the rest of the world.

Chapter 6
Portals Into the Unmanifested

"Your goal is not to battle with the mind, but to witness the mind."

-Swami Muktananda

As previously discussed, spiritual awakening is the beginning of spiritual enlightenment. After you are awakened, you should begin experiencing renewed levels of energy in your body. However, a problem occurs when you can't tap into the energy from your inner self. Most people find it easy to be spiritually awakened. Nevertheless, a problem arises when they begin taking on their journey to enlightenment. This chapter takes a closer look at the portals into the manifested. These are the practical solutions that can help you connect with your inner self.

Going Deep Within Your Body

A major challenge that you could face after spiritually awakening is that you could find it daunting to tap into the energies in your body. To allow your inner energy to flow inside you, you should meditate more often. This doesn't take a lot of time. You can meditate for 10 to 15 minutes. Some people meditate for up to 30 minutes or even an hour. During meditation, you must settle for ideal locations where there is minimal distraction. This should be a room where you are free from digital disturbances or from people.

How you practice your meditation will have an impact on whether you will raise your awareness of the presence of high energy levels in your body. Consequently, you must do it right from the first time.

When practicing breathing exercises, ensure that you assume the right posture and that your body should be fully relaxed. The important thing to confirm during meditation is that you are not thinking about energy flowing inside you. Rather, it should be something that you feel.

Once you draw your attention to the feelings inside you, you can then release any focus object that you were concentrating on. It's imperative that you concentrate entirely on the feeling. After that, you should move in deeper and become one with the feeling. Your oneness with the energy field should connect the inner you and the outer you. Going deeper into your body transcends the body.

You should maintain this state for several minutes as long as you are comfortable. After that, you should bring your attention back to your physical body and your surroundings. Breathe in and out as you gently open your eyes. Such meditation exercise is unmanifested. It frees you from the connection you have with your physical body. In this realm, there is a deeper sense of stillness, peace, love and joy.

The Source of Chi

What is chi (qi)? In the Chinese language, chi is equivalent to breathe. Basically, this is the life force.[18] When you talk in terms of the body, chi distinguishes an alive human being from a corpse. The life force is what makes people alive and present. Stronger and weaker life forces can, therefore, differentiate between two distinct individuals. One with a higher force will be full of life.

---

[18] "What is Chi? - Energy Arts." https://www.energyarts.com/what-is-chi/. Accessed 19 Sep. 2019.

Conversely, an individual with a lesser force will be sluggish or even ill. What this means is that chi—the life force—can be used to cure illness. Ancient Chinese medicine relied on the notion of balancing one's chi to restore the body in a healthy state.[19]

Taoist martial arts such as tai chi, qigong, and other forms of healing arts aid in the development of chi energy. It should be noted that the chi energy developed here is experiential; a feeling that one gains within the body.

Concerning chi being one of the portals into the unmanifested, you can tap into your body's energy source. So, assuming that chi is the energy stream flowing in your body, your goal should be to find the source of that energy flowing in you. This can be achieved through absolute stillness. Achieving stillness is venturing into the unmanifested and going beyond your inner body.

Accordingly, as you take on the path toward connecting with your inner body, there is a likelihood that you can go beyond this stage and tap into the unmanifested. This is a different world than you have been accustomed to. You have a different identity here and you're more conscious than ever before. A sneak peek into the unmanifested reveals to you the reality that you are not made of this world. Yes, you are inseparable from this world, but you are simply different in your own liking.

To make this easier for you to understand, when going about your everyday life, try your best to disconnect from your mind and the rest

---

[19] "What is Chi? - Energy Arts."

of the world. Draw some of your attention to your inner self. Practice to be more aware of your higher inner self in everything that you do. For instance, when relating with other people, bring the inner you to connect with them. Certainly, there is no doubt that people will notice a change in attitude and approach to life when you introduce the real you to the external world.

Other Portals

There are other portals that can take you to the world of the unmanifested. For instance, you can create this portal by shutting down the process of thinking. In a way, this is similar to meditation, but on a higher level. For instance, when looking at a flower, you can choose to focus on the flower to the extent that there is nothing running in your mind at the same time. What this means is that you have created a gap in your mind where no thoughts are coming and going.

Usually, meditation takes a similar form as it tries to notice activity in your mind and trying to control it. The activity in the mind imprisons you and it prevents you from entering into the world of the unmanifested. It thwarts your consciousness to the realization of a higher self inside you.

Besides cessation of thinking, mastering the art of surrendering can also help you venture into the world of the unmanifested. Usually, your inner resistance prevents you from facing reality. It cuts you off from the rest of the world and the people around you. Interestingly, such resistance also separates the real you from yourself. This is your ego taking control of the external you. The more you feel separated, the more you are enslaved to the manifested. This leads to a scenario where you find it difficult to identify yourself. Therefore, it is even harder to connect with your inner self.

The task of finding a way to the unmanifested lies on your shoulders. You have to find a clear path that opens doors to the unmanifested. This begins by connecting with the energy flowing inside you. Find the source of your energy while trying your best to disidentify yourself from your mind. And, more importantly, learn to surrender.

Chapter 7
Kill the Buddha

"If you meet the Buddha on the road, kill him."

- Linji Yixuan

Linji Yixuan, one of the first century's Zen masters, once argued, "If you meet the Buddha on the road, kill him."[20] Without a doubt, this quote sounds controversial since Zen teachings often educate people on how to live better lives. Talking about killing the Buddha raises eyebrows on what Yixuan actually meant. The quote shouldn't be taken literally. First of all, spiritual enlightenment has nothing to do with killing other people. The quote stands as a tool meant to ignite our interrogative abilities with regard to spiritual enlightenment.

Breaking down the quote, the term "road" symbolizes our individual paths to enlightenment. In addition, the term could also be taken to refer to the individual paths that we take toward life. We all have different ways that we prefer as we strive to achieve our goals in life. This is the path that the Zen Master refers to in his quote.

What does the term "Buddha" refer to? "Buddha" symbolizes the perceptions that we have regarding the achievements we get while seeking spiritual enlightenment. Often, when people strive for spiritual awakening or enlightenment, they tend to think that they are better

---

[20] ""If You Meet the Buddha on the Road, Kill Him"." https://fractalenlightenment.com/26323/spirituality/if-you-meet-the-buddha-on-the-road-kill-him. Accessed 19 Sep. 2019.

than other people. The idealized image of perfection is what is referred to by the term "Buddha."

It is not surprising that most people will perceive enlightenment as a path to perfection. Therefore, when they reach a certain point where they think they are good enough, there is a likelihood that they will stop seeking spiritual enlightenment. So, when we talk of Buddha, we symbolize the sense of perfection that we might have in mind. Such perceptions about being perfect ought to be stopped, hence the phrase "kill him."

To attain spiritual enlightenment, it is imperative that we kill the "Buddha" we meet on our spiritual journey. Enlightenment is a continuous experience. One can never argue that there is an end to enlightenment. The experience that you gain will be gradual, and it will improve with time. Accordingly, the main reason why you are encouraged to kill the Buddha is that you shouldn't stop meditating and practicing mindfulness just because you think that you have achieved enlightenment.

You might get to a point where you think you have all it takes to be spiritually enlightened. In addition, when you allow the idealized perfection about enlightenment to get into you, you could end up thinking that you have all the answers. The reality is that even the "answers" that you have must be questioned. Therefore, you need to kill the Buddha and continue meditating. The journey never stops; it only improves with time.

From a practical perspective, it is important for us to understand that our egoic mind could lure us into adopting practices that could make us believe that we are freeing ourselves from suffering. For instance, sometimes blaming other people for our mistakes might appear as a consolation to the errors that we have done. Unfortunately, there is no reward or good feeling gained in such actions. The best thing that you can do is to compassionately kill the Buddha. This means letting go of external perceptions and beliefs that we assume will liberate us from our suffering.

With regard to the external world that we are accustomed to, we should comprehend that there is nothing outside the basic needs that can satisfy our desires. You need to connect with the real you to unveil the purest form of happiness.

Noble Truths from Buddhist Tradition

There are four noble truths that we can learn from the Buddhist tradition. They include:

- Dukkha-The truth of suffering

Buddha teaches us that life is not meant to be smooth. We should recognize the fact that life doesn't settle to our expectations. Humans will aim to cease their sufferings by fulfilling their cravings and desires. However, despite our efforts, satisfaction is never permanent. It is only temporary. The truth about suffering is that regardless of whether we are okay from the outside, we are always unsatisfied.[21]

At first, the Buddhist teaching about the truth of suffering might appear pessimistic. However, Buddhist have a varying understanding in

---

[21] "Religions - Buddhism: The Four Noble Truths - BBC." 17 Nov. 2009, https://www.bbc.co.uk/religion/religions/buddhism/beliefs/fournobletruths_1.shtml. Accessed 19 Sep. 2019.

that they consider it as the reality of things. The good news is that Buddhist teachings also enlighten us on how to end such suffering.

- Samudaya-The origin of suffering

According to Buddha, the source of our suffering goes beyond the worries that we have in mind. The origin of suffering is desire, often termed as *tanha*.[22] *Tanha* comes in three forms including:

- Greed and desire

- Ignorance

- Hatred

- Nirodha- The cessation of suffering

So, how do you free yourself from suffering? Buddha encourages us that the best way of liberating ourselves from pain is by freeing ourselves from attachment.

- Magga-The path to the cessation of suffering

The idea of stopping suffering is something that can be achieved gradually. Based on Buddha's teachings, we can end ou sufferings by following the set of principles commonly referred to as the Eightfold Path.[23] This path includes such concepts as right understanding, intention, speech, action, livelihood, effort, mindfulness, and right concentration.

---

[22] "Religions - Buddhism: The Four Noble Truths - BBC."

[23] "Religions - Buddhism: The Four Noble Truths - BBC."

Piia Rauha

Concerning the notion of killing the Buddha, we shouldn't be blinded by external things thinking that they can end our suffering. Life is full of pain; this is the reality that we have to face. People should comprehend that striving to achieve worldly desires doesn't lead to true happiness. Pleasure is only temporary. To stop ourselves from suffering, the best thing that we can do is to liberate ourselves from the attachment we have with our desires.

Chapter 8
Right Here, Right Now!

"The past is a ghost, the future a dream and all we ever have is now."

-Bill Cosby

When you look at the world around us, it is quite noticeable that we are either thinking about the past or the future. People have blamed the challenges of life as the main reason why they can't live in the present. Certainly, this doesn't mean that thinking about the past and the future is a bad thing. Without a doubt, we all need to visualize sometimes. However, it is worth noting that you can also access your past and your future by simply living in the present moment. This chapter aims to help you understand that there is power in living in the present moment. It will outline essential tips that can help you enhance your awareness of the world around you. More importantly, you will learn about the benefits of developing higher awareness.

When Are You Present? When Are You Not?

To clearly understand the significance of living in the present, it is imperative that you draw a thick line between the times when you are present and those that you aren't. When you are not living in the present, it means that you are a victim of time.[24] Often, you will notice that your mind constantly drifts either to the past or to the future or

---

[24] "Present Moment - Pocket Mindfulness." https://www.pocketmindfulness.com/live-in-the-present-moment/. Accessed 20 Sep. 2019.

even both. As previously mentioned, it is not a bad thing to think about the past and the future. The issue is that when your life is dictated by what happened in the past or what you think will happen in the near future, it becomes challenging for you to live in the present.

The routine that you might develop is to think negatively about what had happened before and that it could also affect your future. Similarly, you could develop a habit where your future makes you anxious. Rarely, you are here and now to enjoy life. The worst thing about the habits that we develop is that they become a norm. With time, you will find that you cannot determine whether something is wrong because you are used to doing it.

To easily break away from being a victim of time, you first need to comprehend the meaning of time. Simply stated, time is a human concept.[25] Naturally, time wasn't time. Humans came up with a way of monitoring how they spend their lives using time. Mother nature doesn't understand time. To mother nature, life is simply evolving. The reality is that time doesn't exist. The concept of time only drives us into concentrating on events that have passed and those that are coming. The problem with this is that we never stop to enjoy the moment. For instance, instead of enjoying the time you spend with your family over the weekend, your mind might get consumed with the deadlines you have on Monday.

---

[25] "Present Moment - Pocket Mindfulness."
https://www.pocketmindfulness.com/live-in-the-present-moment/. Accessed 20 Sep. 2019.

Allowing yourself to be a victim of time only has negative consequences on your life. You will always be a slave to your past and the future. This means that your life will always be filled with uneasiness. This will make you vulnerable to some of the things that we are trying to overcome in today's world, including agitation, stress, anxiety, and depression.

The Power of Presence

Do you remember the last time you engaged in a healthy conversation without allowing your mind to drift and think about other things? Without a doubt, there are numerous times when we find ourselves absent from the present moment. This is because we allow distractions to prevent us from knowing what it means to be really alive. Usually, we are fixated with thoughts about our past or the future.

There is power in living in the present. Mahatma Gandhi once said, "The future depends on what you do today." Indeed, being in the present is what determines how your future will be. Setting goals and working toward a brighter future occurs in the present. Time is just an illusion; you have the power to shape your future if you choose to live in the present. Accordingly, if you choose to live more in the present, then there is a chance that your future will also be good.

Developing Higher Awareness

Now that you know there is power in living in the present, you must understand how to enhance your consciousness. The first thing that you ought to do is to have the intention that you need to be more aware of being in the present. In addition, meditation will help you train your mind on where to focus on. Meditation practices will guarantee that you can monitor your thoughts and know when they are drifting a lot into the past or the future.

Developing a higher state of awareness also requires that you focus on your body. Your physical body is the only tool you have to help you live your life. As such, you must enhance your awareness by taking good care of it. This means eating the right foods and exercising regularly.

Practicing self-control will also help you develop a higher state of consciousness. You must monitor how you behave and react to certain things. By mastering your reactions, you can determine whether what you are doing is right or wrong. This allows you to change for the better. Self-control centers around feelings, thoughts, actions, and speech. These are the things that you should monitor in your life.

Undeniably, success in life comes as a result of the knowledge that you acquire as you continue living your life. Your self-knowledge will improve as you continue evaluating your strengths and weaknesses. Just like reading this book, you unlock your potential to uncovering the divine being inside you. Indeed, this also enhances your levels of consciousness.

Besides, your level of consciousness will also be given a considerable boost if you master how to discipline your mind. This demands that you clear the clutter in your mind. Without a clear mind, you will not think straight. Thoughts and feelings will always seem to overwhelm you. A mind, free from clutter, will be free from distractions, fears, and worries. This means that you will be in a better position to value the importance of being here and now.

Everyday Benefits of Developing Higher Awareness

Numerous benefits will come your way when you develop a higher state of awareness. Some of them are discussed as follows.

Realize Life's Greater Purpose

Frankly, life can be unfair and chaotic sometimes. This happens because of what we choose to focus on. Today, most of us are consumed by the hustle and bustle of our everyday lives. You can't help to think about doing the job that you hate. You find yourself worrying too much about your financial status.

A higher state of awareness helps you to take control of your life. You begin to open your eyes to the realization that certain things are beyond your control. So, you start working on what you can control. The beauty of this is that you learn to surrender what you can't manage. This paves the way to a more fulfilling life.

Higher Levels of Intuition

With enhanced levels of awareness, you will also develop high intuition levels that guide you in making smart decisions about your life. You will be more at peace with your inner self. This means that you will have faith in yourself. As a result, second-guessing will gradually diminish.

An Enhancement in Your Natural Abilities

Bearing in mind that you will be more confident with yourself, this means that you will find it easy to learn and develop new skills in your life. The high level of consciousness that you will be operating on will ensure that you don't waste your energy on the unimportant things in life. For instance, you will understand that there is no joy in fulfilling your external desires. Therefore, you will want to focus more on building yourself from the inside. This includes working on your talent and honing your abilities.

Emotional Intelligence

When you are more conscious about who you are, you will find it easy to deal with your emotions. You understand yourself better, and this will influence your relationship with people. Often, you will strive to ensure that your feelings do not get the best of you. In addition, you will have a deeper understanding of your strengths and weaknesses. Therefore, you will know how to manage your emotions in a way that they don't affect your everyday life.

Stronger Relationships

Following your personal development, this also leads to better and healthier relationships with other people. People will see you as a different and approachable person. They will always appreciate your presence and would love to know you more. This is because they also feel the energy that flows within you. The good news is that your self-awareness will also help you to solve relationship issues that you might face from time to time.

Attraction of Wealth and Abundance

Of course, living a conscious life doesn't mean that you will become rich quickly. However, you can be certain that you will grow wealthier. This happens because of your strong belief that you are full of potential. The feeling that you are unstoppable will drive you to strive for higher limits in your career.

What's more, your mind will also rise above basic thinking. Naturally, you will start thinking of more significant things that are worth achieving in life. This fills you with abundance in everything that you do.

You will live a life of optimism. This will have an impact on what you choose to do with your career and all areas of your life. Accordingly, you will often feel as though everything is falling into place in your life.

In summary, there is more to life than just thinking about the past and the future. Sure, thinking about your past and the near future doesn't count as a bad thing. However, you ought to realize that such thinking hinders you from enjoying life. The true meaning of life is realized when you choose to live in the present. It is also worth mentioning that being in the present is what counts most. Your future is mainly dependent on what you do now. So, there is no need to waste your energy worrying about what could be. Work now, focus on the present and let the future worry about itself.

Chapter 9
Feelings and Emotions:
Understanding the Difference

"One can be the master of what one does, but never of what one feels."

— *Gustave Flaubert*

Usually, the terms feelings and emotions are used interchangeably. What people fail to realize is that the two terms are distinct. Although people might understand what we are saying, it is still imperative that we draw a distinction between the two terms. It is through this understanding that people can find peace and happiness in their lives.

What are Emotions?

Emotions refer to responses that occur in the amygdala and ventromedial prefrontal cortices sections of the brain.[26] Originally, emotions helped ancient species to survive. The notion of reacting fast to threats and other things surrounding their wild environments helped people to survive. Emotional reactions vary slightly from one individual to the other and also to other animals. Regardless, it can be pointed out that emotional responses are universally similar. For instance, when

---

[26] "What's The Difference Between Feelings And Emotions? - The ...." 12 Jan. 2015, https://www.thebestbrainpossible.com/whats-the-difference-between-feelings-and-emotions/. Accessed 20 Sep. 2019.

you smile at your dog, your dog notices the happy mood and it wags its tail.

Some of the common emotions that are universally recognized include grief, fear, rage, love, anger, disgust, happiness, and sadness.[27] Emotions precede feelings. In addition, they are instinctual and physical. Due to their physical attributes, emotions can be objectively measured through the brain's activity, blood flow, body language, or facial micro-expressions.

What are Feelings?

Feelings are mental reactions to emotions. They are acquired via experience. When people talk about feelings, they usually jump to talk about emotions because emotions are universal. The feelings that you go through are colored by memories and thoughts that you have subconsciously linked with a specific emotion. For instance, when you think about something scary, this can evoke a fear response. Emotions triggered might linger for a short while. However, feelings triggered as a result of those emotions could last for a lifetime. The main reason why this happens is that emotions trigger subconscious feelings. The effect of this is that emotional response is also created.

The problem here is that if you fail to control your feelings, your life can be clouded with never-ending emotions. You will suffer the burden of dealing with these emotions in your life. Negative emotions

---

[27] "Feelings And Emotions - Laughter Online University."
https://www.laughteronlineuniversity.com/feelings-and-emotions/. Accessed 20 Sep. 2019.

will weigh you down. You will find life stressful since you are never happy.

When seeking spiritual awakening and enlightenment, it is important that you understand your emotions and feelings. This is because these feelings and emotions determine how you interact with the world. Certainly, these emotions have a huge impact on how people behave and relate to other people. The aspect of living unconsciously about your feelings and emotions could lead to problems and numerous life challenges. This is for the reasons that fear-based perceptions might evoke particular feelings that might negatively affect your life.

Emotions and Feelings: Putting the Difference in Good Use

Understanding the difference between emotions and feelings will definitely help you to navigate the challenges that this world has to offer. In addition, living consciously about these feelings and emotions helps you to grow into a better individual. For example, you will be in a better position to determine when to react and when to respond to a particular situation. Your actions will be heavily reliant on how well you comprehend your feelings and emotions.

Without a doubt, gaining knowledge about feelings and emotions is just not enough to guarantee that you navigate this chaotic world with ease. No! The point here is that you should understand the difference between the two and change your behavior and attitude toward life. In this case, you should acknowledge the fact that no matter what happens, you are always in control of your actions. Accordingly, you will live a purposeful life full of peace.

You Are Not Always Aware of Your Emotions

The reason why we are stressing on emotional awareness is that you are often unaware of these emotions. Most people are engrossed by their emotions in the same way a fish is immersed in water. The feelings surrounding them influence who they are and the type of persons that they choose to be. The worst thing is that the lack of awareness makes it challenging for people to turn over a new leaf. If one is engrossed in negative emotions, it means that they live and breathe negativity. Sometimes you might even think that these individuals were born that way because there is nothing else that they know of.

So, how can one become aware of the kind of emotions that they are consumed with? Here, an ideal strategy to utilize will be taking on the observer's role. We have talked about this previously. Just to remind you, taking on the role of an observer in your life means looking at yourself from a different perspective. Besides observing your thoughts, you can also observe your emotions. Ideally, giving your emotions a second thought can help to gauge whether your reaction is worth it or not. You can then avoid reacting altogether and find a better strategy to approach your problem. Without a doubt, doing this ensures that you rarely or never fuss with other people. This is because you will be operating on a higher level of consciousness where you know that some things are just not worth your reaction.

Our Attraction To Emotions

It is also worth questioning why people are usually attracted to certain emotions. The truth about this is that people will yearn to experience specific emotions more than others. Individuals spend the better part of their lives trying their best to attain certain states that will make them feel particular emotions. For example, there are good emotions associated with achieving goals and living your dream.

Typically, individuals will search for spiritual or heart-based emotions. Some of these emotions include feeling happy, being in love, feeling joyful, peaceful, and so on. Similarly, a good number of people will search for ego-based emotions. Examples of these emotions are feeling superior or powerful. We live in a world where we are accustomed to people trying their best to be better than others. The ego-based emotions drive us into thinking that we are in a competition. True happiness is not gained by satisfying out egos. We realize this later in life after achieving all that we had hoped for. Ultimately, our eyes are opened to the realization that material/external things lead to temporary happiness.

Perhaps the world would have been a better place is most people valued heart-based emotions over ego-based emotions. We would place high value for love over the quest for money. People would prioritize experiences over material possessions. In as much as this might sound out of the ordinary, it is nothing but the truth.

The attraction that people have toward emotions shouldn't be taken for granted. This is because some people get addicted to their emotions. Most people will search for ego-based emotions strongly to the extent where they are addicted or obsessed. Some of the emotions that we are talking about here include emotions originating from addiction to gambling, money, and power. Physical sensations from cigarettes, drugs, and alcohol also fall under this category.

A major challenge that people face when these emotions overwhelm them is that they lose control. This happens because such emotions generate strong addictive energy that is difficult to ignore. At this point, addicts find it daunting to say no. The aftermath is that the emotions could control how addicts think and behave.

5-Step Approach to Control Unwanted Emotions

Unwanted emotions can weigh you down in ways that you never anticipated. Following what we have discussed about emotions and feelings, it is important that you learn how to control unwanted emotions. By controlling these emotions, it also means that you will control how you behave toward other people when these emotions ensue. The following is a 5-step approach that you should embrace to help you deal with unwanted emotions.

Step 1: Select the Situation

The idea here is that you should try your best to avoid situations that could trigger unwanted emotions. For instance, if you are the type of person who gets angry when in a rush, you should consider doing things at the right time. Avoid situations that could make you delay with what you were trying to do. Concerning your friends and other relationships, maybe there is a person that you find annoying. The right way of ensuring that such people don't ruin your moods is by avoiding them.

Step 2: Modify the Situation

You can also opt to modify the situation as a remedy to prevent unwanted feelings from overwhelming you. Say you always feel that you are disappointed over certain things, e.g., cooking for your family and friends. Your disappointment could be as a result of trying too hard. Chances are that you aim too high, and this makes you disappointed when you don't meet your targets. In such cases, the best solution is to modify the situation. Try to settle for something that works with you. It doesn't have to be something huge. If you are planning to cook, simply go for recipes that are readily available and that you are an expert in what you are trying to prepare.

Step 3: Shift Your Focus

Sometimes ego-based emotions such as jealousy could crush you because you are focusing in the wrong direction. Most people endeavor to get rich. This makes them to compare themselves with some of their rich friends. The problem with this is that individuals end up getting frustrated with their efforts. As such, most of them end up giving up because they can't outshine or live fancy lives like other people.

The same thing happens to people who hit the gym for the first time. Usually, you will find that beginners are psyched up to train, lose weight, and shred their bodies just like the individuals they envision at the gym. Instead of finding motivation from physically fit folks at the gym, they often get discouraged. Negative emotions get the best of them as they assume that they still have a long way to go.

Therefore, it is important that you shift your attention and focus on something that can motivate you. When striving to lose weight, find a group of friends who have similar goals. This can help you build your confidence since you will be competing with individuals in your own level.

Step 4: Change Your Thoughts

Basically, our emotions are driven by our thoughts. If you are thinking about all the great things that have happened in your life, you will evoke emotions of happiness and joy. Conversely, if you are musing over past events that have affected your life negatively, you will trigger sad feelings.

Therefore, the best path that you can take to prevent unwanted emotions from overwhelming you is by changing your thoughts. Sure, you might not change the situation, but you will have altered your perceptions about that which affects how you feel. Rather than thinking about things that will make you sad, shift your thinking and reflect on things or events that will make you happy.

Step 5: Change Your Response

There is a possibility that the above steps might fail to work. Some of the emotions that we experience are too strong for us to bear. So, what should you do when these emotions seem uncontrollable. Your last approach will be to change your response. Maybe you are feeling angry and that you are about to explode and punch someone that wronged you. Don't be fast to react. Take a few deep breaths to calm yourself. Give yourself some time to think about what you are about to do and the repercussions that could ensue. Changing your response will change the entire ordeal. There is a likelihood that you will settle for a more reasonable move.

To sum this up, feelings and emotions can come in the way of being enlightened. For that reason, it is essential that you understand how to control your emotions. By being aware of your emotions, you are better placed to make informed decisions about your life. In this case, you will know how to interact peacefully and consciously with people around you. What's more, you will navigate through this chaotic life without allowing ego-based emotions to drive your actions.

Chapter 10
The Importance of Surrendering

"Some of us think holding on makes us strong; but sometimes it is letting go."

-Hermann Hesse

When we talk of surrendering, you might be thinking in the negative direction thinking that we are trying to discourage you from fighting and dealing with life's challenges. Surrendering truly is something different altogether. Spiritually speaking true surrendering refers to the process of yielding to a certain situation instead of opposing it. When we talk about life, most people will try to oppose the flow of life. Regardless of the fact that you understand that some things are beyond your control, you will try to force things to work. In such instances, you are only opposing the flow of life.

Accepting The Now

The flow of life can only be experienced once you choose to live in the present moment. Here, you will begin to see life from a different perspective since you understand that some things are better left as they are. With this mentality, you will surrender to what life is. Without judgement, you will want to surrender unconditionally to everything that is happening in your life now. This kind of surrendering gives you a reason to overcome the inner resistance that might be telling you to say no. Your egoic mind might lure you through negative perceptions to believe that your life is determined by your past or your future.

Therefore, overcoming this resistance is what we refer to as the process of accepting the now.

Individuals with experience of life can say a lot about the fact that things never turn out as we expect. When you choose to uphold the value of surrendering, you will realize that you can free yourself from emotional and physical pain. Such acceptance of what life is all about eliminates pain from your life. There is nothing bad in letting go. It only means that you are strong enough to understand that there is more to life than trying to control that which is beyond your power. Notably, one of the main importance of surrendering is that it helps to disidentify yourself from your mind. As such, you connect more your true nature, which is your being.

An interesting thing that should come to your attention is that surrendering to the now is similar to taking action and living your life as you want. The only difference is that surrendering takes on a different energy. It can be said that surrendering connects you to your chi. Since your action will be connected to your true self, this will evoke joy, happiness and bliss. Ultimately, your consciousness will be greatly improved and you will notice that this is something that you can achieve with minimal effort. The positive energy flowing in you will have a profound impact on all aspects of your life. People will admire you. They will see the glow in you and will want to associate with you. Have you ever noticed that there are those people who tend to attract a large following due to their intelligence? Well, this will also happen to you.

Moving From Mind Energy To Spiritual Energy

The notion of letting go is not as easy as you might think. Regardless, it is something that you can achieve. At times you will feel the resistance from your mind that you don't have to let go. Ideally, this is the best place to start your campaign and master the art of surrendering. Start by admitting that your mind is resisting this change. You should be aware of this resistance and become present when it happens. Take the role of the observer and note how your mind is developing the resistance. Observe how the mind is perceiving the situation and mull over other thoughts that flow to your mind as it resists change.

It is through witnessing the mind resisting such desired surrendering that you will realize that there is no reason to resist. You will awaken the unconscious resistance and this is where you win over your mind.

Surrendering in Personal Relationships

The concept of surrendering is also applicable in personal relationships. We live in a world where there are those people who will try and control or manipulate you. These are individuals who live unconsciously. The main reason why they will want to manipulate you is because they want to use your energy for their own benefit. Instead of fighting them, you should surrender. Of course, this doesn't mean that you allow other people to exploit you. The idea here is that you should learn how to say "no" without being offensive. In addition, walking away from the situation can also make a huge difference. It prevents you from having to consider the chances of being manipulated by a friend or any other person.

Surrendering will help enhance the quality of your relationships. You will welcome people into your life because you understand them in ways that they can't explain. The mere fact that you will be surrendering to them shows that you can live with their weaknesses without being judgmental. Indeed, this is a quality that most people lack. Usually, it hinders individuals from appreciating other people without judging or criticizing them.

Changing Your Suffering Into Peace

When people suffer or go through pain in their lives, their immediate reaction is to cut themselves off from their feelings. Without doubt, this is something that we cannot assume. We are often faced with the dilemma of facing our struggles or simply giving up. Unfortunately, giving up is not always an option. Moreover, the notion of ignoring our feelings also doesn't help save the situation.

Surrendering can also help save you from suffering. Certainly, you must be wondering how surrendering can be helpful as it would appear as though you are giving up. One thing that you should understand is that surrendering is not the same as giving up. When you choose to surrender, it means that you are acknowledging the fact that there are certain things which are beyond your control. Therefore, instead of fighting the reality of now, you choose to accept it. The advantage gained here is that you free yourself from suffering. You will be at peace with yourself since you choose to live in the present by accepting things as they are.

So, living in a state of acceptance to all that happens around you creates an environment where you are free from negativity. Negative energy will not flow in you since you are pretty convinced that everything happens for a reason. This means that you will live in a world full of happiness and bliss. Therefore, surrendering is not a weakness. You should not perceive the concept of surrendering from a negative perspective. From the information discussed, there is power in surrendering and accepting things as they are.

The end... almost!

Reviews are not easy to come by.

As an independent author with a tiny marketing budget, I rely on readers, like you, to leave a short review on Amazon.

Even if it's just a sentence or two!

So if you enjoyed the book, please...

>> Click here to leave a brief review on Amazon.

https://www.amazon.com/review/create-review?asin=B0817TB7MQ

I am very appreciative for your review as it truly makes a difference.

Thank you from the bottom of my heart for purchasing this book and reading it to the end.

Final Thoughts

Congratulations on reaching this final section of this book. Arguably, there is a lot that you have learned concerning spiritual enlightenment. The good news is that you are now convinced that spiritual enlightenment is not far from your reach just as you had previously thought. Sure, the journey to spiritual enlightenment begins with spiritual awakening. First, you have to open your eyes to the realization that you have been dreaming all this time. Chances are that your mind has been controlling you. Your lack of awareness might have made you believe that gaining motivation to meet your career goals will make you happy.

Now, you have the knowledge and power to discern where true happiness emanates from. True happiness comes from within. To understand this in depth, it requires a high level of awareness that you have to build. Usually, people are blinded from the reality of life because they allow their minds to control them. The most important thing that you should comprehend is that you are not your mind. In fact, based on what this book has outlined, the mind is the greatest obstacle to spiritual enlightenment.

Most people identify themselves with their minds because they are not conscious of their thoughts. The compulsive thoughts that are always rushing in our minds create a barrier between you and your true self. In your ordinary day, chances are that your mind will be filled with plans of how you will manage your day. From morning, you will try to manage your to-do list while at the same time juggling with other pressures of life. Unfortunately, all this creates an opaque frame preventing us from realizing our true self. You might end up working for the next twenty years without giving yourself some time to enjoy yourself.

Indeed, this is the life that most people are living out there. Their 9 to 5 jobs are holding them captives. What people fail to realize is that their hard-earned money doesn't buy them happiness. Well, of course, the idea here is not to discourage you from doing your best to earn money and support your family and your career. Certainly not! The point is that you should raise your awareness to comprehend that your egoic mind might make you believe that getting money is the path to true happiness. For that reason, you ought to learn and master the art of disidentifying yourself from your mind.

Disidentifying yourself from your mind is not something that is beyond your reach. In fact, you can learn how to control your mind by listening to your inner voice. We all have this inner voice that keeps talking to us about the things that we should and shouldn't do. Sometimes we make the wrong decisions because we choose to listen to our mind without taking a higher authority and consulting our inner voice. Practicing to listen to your inner voice raises your consciousness about the thoughts and emotions inside your mind. For instance, your mind might steer away from a get together event that you were having with your family. When you are conscious about your thoughts, you can easily bring back your mind to the present moment.

An ideal strategy that can help you control your mind is assuming the role of an observer. Here, you observe "the thinker." The mind tends to act independently since it has a mind of its own. Observing your mind impartially gives you a higher authority over it. You gain a higher level of awareness, which guarantees that you can stop yourself from thinking in a particular direction. This means that by controlling your thoughts, you also control the direction your life takes. An important thing that you should remember when using the observer's strategy is that you should not judge or criticize your thoughts. Your role is just to observe and be aware.

It is quite sad that most people we encounter in our lives go through life with pain and regrets. Why do people live their lives feeling bitter, angry, and resentful? Well, people have created certain perceptions about a beautiful life that they crave to live. Most of them refer to this life as the "American dream." When people fail to live their lives as they had anticipated, they become more stressed, depressed and frustrated. Truly, just as Buddha teachings informed us, the source of pain is greed and desire. Additionally, our suffering could be as a result of the hatred that we have allowed to grow in us. Moreover, we are ignorant to reality and this makes us to suffer even more.

As people try their best to eliminate pain in their lives, they use the wrong strategies for welcoming happiness and bliss in their lives. Millions of people believe in material things. They place high regard to material things and forget to reflect inside themselves to find true happiness. We all have examples of rich people who died because of depression. Sometimes we have also been victims of trying to attain happiness through material things. In the end, we realize that happiness and joy from the external world is temporary. This book explains to us why happiness from within is worth striving for.

When you talk of living in pain, people also experience pain because they choose to live in their past. Many at times you will find individuals feeling sad because they remember certain things that happened decades ago. We should understand that time is just an illusion. What happened in the past happened. The most important thing in life is to live in the present. Ruminating about your past will only invite negative feelings that will weigh you down. There is no need for you to torture yourself by focusing too much on what happened in the past.

Another major issue worth talking about is the notion of paying too much attention on the future. Just like focusing on your past, focusing too much on your future also prevents you from living in the present. You will end up wasting a lot of energy thinking about what could be. In addition, you will be anxious about events that you cannot control. Living in the past and the future only deters you from living your life. You will never understand the true meaning of life if you never stop and live in the present.

Think about this; there is power in being here and now. What you are going to do today will determine how your future will be. This should open your eyes to understand that the only time you have is now. You can only change what you can and should do now. However, you have no control over your past and the future. So, why waste your time trying to change something that you can't. At least you can change what you can do now. Therefore, it makes a lot of sense if you paid attention to living in the moment.

Let's be honest, we live in a chaotic world where it might be challenging to live in the present. Bearing this in mind, there are certain exercises that you should embrace to enhance your awareness muscles. For example, practicing mindfulness can be a great way of bringing your mind to the present. This is something that you can easily practice with your everyday activities. When you are washing the dishes, instead of allowing your mind to think about your past or worry about the future, pay attention to the sound of the dishes as they come into contact with the sink. How cold is the water? Again, mindfulness meditation can be practiced when you are walking. Raise your awareness about your thoughts by choosing to focus on what you are seeing when walking down the streets. This can be the color of the shops that you are coming across or the beautiful people that you are interacting with on the way. These simple cues can make a huge difference toward increasing your consciousness.

With regard to enhancing your consciousness, you should also embark on awakening your third eye. Remember, enlightenment is more of an experience where you learn more about yourself. You enter into a realm where you discover that you are not who you thought you were. You connect with your higher self and this leads you to a path of spiritual enlightenment. This is an individual experience and therefore, the experience that another individual goes through will be distinct from yours.

Another thing worth reminding you about is exploiting the portals of the unmanifested. These are practical solutions that you can rely on to connect with your inner self. The most important thing that you need to understand here is that you only need to rely on one portal that can connect you to your inner self. The method you choose should work for you. One of such portals is finding your source of chi. This is the energy that flows in you. Where does this energy come from? Identifying your source of chi helps you to tap into your body's energy source. The significance of finding the source of your chi is that it takes you beyond your higher self. Therefore, you will be taken to another realm where you are in a state of high consciousness beyond your understanding.

Similarly, meditation is a practical portal that you can open to the world of the unmanifested. Practicing meditation will help you control your mind. Thoughts and emotions in your mind can deter you from entering into the world of the unmanifested. Therefore, by controlling the direction of your thoughts, there is a good chance that you will use this portal to connect with the real you.

The journey to spiritual enlightenment never ends. You will always improve on the skills that you gain toward improving your self-awareness. At no point should you think that you have achieved enlightenment. Kill the Buddha when you reach a point where you think that you are better than ever before. Spiritually speaking, you should get it clear that enlightenment is not a path to perfection. Rather, it is a path to self-discovery. The real you never changes regardless of what happens. So, don't stop meditating and practicing mindfulness. Continue equipping yourself with knowledge that will help you transform into the person that the inner you will admire. Choosing to read this book, for example, was a wise move that has changed how you feel about yourself. Undeniably, you are not your mind.

Last but not least, always bear in mind that there are numerous benefits of developing higher awareness. There is a huge reward that you will gain by doing what you can to live mindfully. First, you will have higher levels of intuition. Secondly, you will live a life with a greater purpose. That's not all, you will give a huge boost to your emotional intelligence since you will learn how to best control your emotions. You will value the relationships you share with other people since you share with them the love that emanates from inside you. More importantly, you will attract wealth and abundance your way.

Good luck!

DOWNLOAD YOUR FREE GIFT BELOW:

Go from Stress to Success with These 15 Powerful Tips

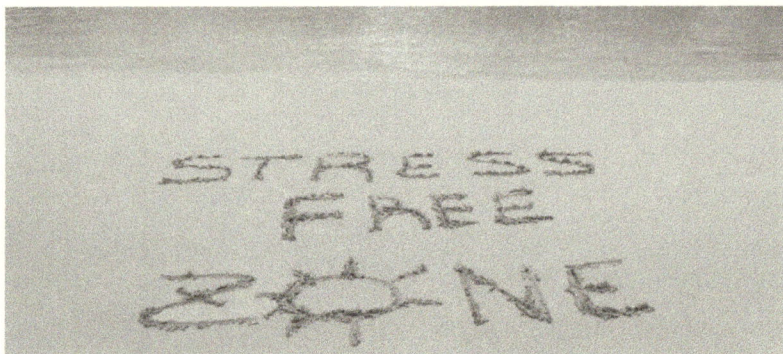

You're in The Tunnel, Now Turn on The Light:

Here are The Best Ways to Transform Your Success

Do You Feel Stressed-Out, Overwhelmed and Harassed Every Day?

Then you're stuck in a negative thought spiral that is keeping you from achieving *real success!*

How many times have you thought, 'if only I could be more productive, then I'd get ahead?' No matter how hard you try, it eludes you. Most people experience intense self-doubt, worry and negative thinking at some point in their careers. These are your immediate obstacles to success.

This guide tackles these issues with easy, direct solutions to help you break the cycle and get back on track. These 15 powerful tips will take you from overwhelmed to overjoyed, in no time!

This FREE Cheat Sheet contains:

- Essential tips on how to stop worrying and start living

- How to actually relieve anxiety and banish it for good

- Ways to get rid of negative thoughts, and how to stop them from recurring

- Tips to become the most productive, motivated version of yourself

- How to focus on career success and build positive cycles and habits

Scroll down and click the link **below to Claim your Free Cheat Sheet!**

I want you to know that you don't have to live this way. You don't have to feel like these negative cycles are getting the better of you. Your career is waiting to bloom – and flourish! Give yourself the opportunity to make the right choices, by learning how to authentically reach for lasting success.

Ditch the stress, embrace success.

Click Here!

Check out our Other *AMAZING* Titles

Book 1: <u>Buddhism for Beginners</u>

<u>The Path to Liberation &</u>

<u>Enlightenment</u>

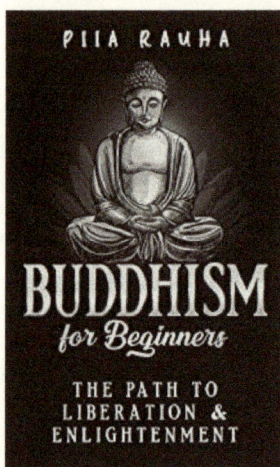

Without a doubt, the most important pilgrimage sites are located in modern-day India but several others were built centuries after Buddha's passing by a number of his patrons. The spread of Buddhism across Asia speaks of its universal message that every human being can relate to, regardless of race, religion, and culture.

Buddhism believes in love and respect for all creatures

For the reader, the list of pilgrimage sites compiled here serves as information for true seekers of Buddhism. Quite clearly, one should take visiting any of these sites seriously if one must honor centuries of Buddhist tradition that has passed on from generation to generation as it spread across Asia.

As we learned earlier, the Buddha instructed his disciples to visit these pilgrimage sites as a way of demonstrating their commitment toward the faith known as Buddhism. So, without further ado, let us look at the eight most important sites but also other pilgrimage sites across Asia that receive a large number of visitors who wish to honor the life and work of the Buddha.

The Eight Important Buddhist Pilgrimage Sites

Since the Buddha attained enlightenment and preached through the length and breadth of India, the most important Buddhist pilgrimage sites are located in the Indian subcontinent. Right from his place of birth to where he breathed his last. As he had instructed his disciples to not only visit these places but also distribute relics after his cremation, there are a number of other sites that are considered holy to those who practice Buddhism.

Buddha Carving in Thailand

But let us look at the eight most important pilgrimage sites first before we look at a number of others that have also gained prominence long after the Buddha breathed his last and attained 'nirvana'.

Birth – Lumbini, Nepal

As most Buddhists already know, Siddhartha was born in Lumbini that is located in modern-day Nepal. It is well-known for being located at the foot of the Himalayan mountains. Pilgrims visit the Maya Devi Temple which is considered to be the birthplace temple and is named after Buddha's mother who passed after giving birth to him.

Birthplace of the Buddha – Lumbini, Nepal

With a number of pilgrims visiting the site each year, the Shanti Gumba and the Ashokan Pillar are also worth visiting apart from the Buddhist monasteries that mark Lumbini's landscape. However, this isn't a sacred site for Buddhists only since the Hindus also revere Siddhartha Gautama and are known to visit the place of his birth with equal fervor.

Enlightenment – Body Gaya, India

After six years of practicing extreme asceticism, the Buddha was said to have attained enlightenment under a pipal tree that came to be known as the Bodhi tree. It was in honor of this event that the Indian Emperor Ashoka built the Mahabodhi Temple.

Mahabodhi Temple in Bodh Gaya, India

Of course, while the tree under which the Siddhartha attained enlightenment does not live to tell the tale, the tree that currently exists in the Mahabodhi Temple Complex is a direct descendant of that very 'pipal' tree. In fact, a sapling was taken from the Bodhi tree and taken to Sri Lanka, which, in turn, is a descendant from the tree under which the Buddha found enlightenment.

First Sermon – Sarnath, India

Sarnath, which is located in modern-day Uttar Pradesh in India, is the place where the Buddha gave his first sermon along with also setting up the Buddhist sangha. Legend has it that this was the place where the five ascetics achieved 'arhathood'. As we already know, the five ascetics that he had sought enlightenment with became his disciples when he met them at the deer park.

Dhamek Stupa at Sarnath

Built by Emperor Ashoka, this stupa is located at the exact spot where the Buddha gave his very first sermon on the Four Noble Truths. Another notable monument in the area includes the Lion Capital of Ashoka that was built by Emperor Ashoka as well. Apart from this, not only will you find the Dharmachakra Stupa but also an image of Buddha and a temple built by the Tibetan community too.

'Mahaparinirvana' or passing – Kushinagar, India

Considered to be an important pilgrimage site for Buddhists all over the world, Kushinagar is the place where, according to most modern scholars, the Buddha breathed his last. The Ramabhar stupa was built over a part of Buddha's ashes. As one can tell, this is the exact location of where the Buddha was cremated.

The Ramabhar Stupa in Kushinagar

As a part of Buddhist beliefs, this was also the location where he attained 'parinirvana' as well and which is home to the Nirvana stupa. Along with this, the Mahaparinirvana temple was also built at Kushinagar in 1956 and which houses the 6.1 meter Dying Buddha statue. This statue shows the Buddha reclining on his right and looking to the west. The Matha Kuar Shrine is also found at this location.

Where He First Started as a Monk – Rajagaha, India

Considered to be the capital of the Magadha kings, this city is known for its ties with both Buddhism and Jainism. The Buddha began his journey to enlightenment at this location and which is why it is also an important pilgrimage site for the Buddhists.

Gridhra-kuta Hill of the Vultures

In fact, after attaining 'nirvana', he spent several months at Rajagaha meditating and preaching important sermons to his disciples. Another reason why this location is so important is that it was the location for the First Convocation of the Buddhist council right after the Buddha's passing.

Where He Rested During the Rainy Seasons – Shravasti, India

This ancient city is found along the banks of the Rapti river in modern-day Uttar Pradesh in India. This was where the Buddha spent 24 rainy seasons of his life. The reason why this location is also an important pilgrimage site for the Buddhists is that it is believed that the Buddha spent the most amount of time in his adult life at this location.

Miracle of Shravasti

Of the 24 rainy seasons that he spent here, 19 were spent at the Jetavana monastery while the remaining 6 were spent at the Pubbarama monastery. It was at this location that the Buddha also performed the Twin Miracle of emitting both water and fire from his body. What is also important about this location is the Angulimala stupa that is located in Shravasthi too.

Where He Descended to Earth from Tusita Heaven – Sankassa, India

Despite being a hard-to-reach pilgrimage site, Sankassa is said to be the place where the Buddha returned to earth after completing his sermons found in the Abhidhamma Pitaka at Tavatimsa. This city is located in modern-day Uttar Pradesh in India and where the Emperor Ashoka built a number of Buddhist temples and stupas. One of these temples has been dedicated to the mother of the Buddha otherwise known as Vishari Devi.

Depiction of the Descent by the Buddha at Sankassa

In fact, it is said that all Buddhas descend to earth at this very site after preaching the Abhidhamma. According to the pilgrims Faxian and Xuanzang, three ladders were found at this site to commemorate the descent of the Buddha.

Where He Preached His Last Sermon – Vaishali, India

Located in modern-day Bihar in India, this Buddhist pilgrimage site is considered important as it was the place where the Buddha preached his last sermon after attaining enlightenment. In fact, before this life-changing event, he had stayed in Vaishali to receive training from respected teachers too.

The Ashoka Pillar at Vaishali

Of utmost importance are the ruins of the Kutagarasala Vihara where the Buddha stayed during his visits. But what makes this city a significant one for Buddhists is the fact that it was in this city that he revealed his final departure from the world. It would also mark the final rainy season that he spent in this world. Also, the city is also remembered for hosting the Second Buddhist Council and for being home to one of the best-preserved Ashokan pillars constructed during his reign.

Other Pilgrimage Sites Across South-East Asia

While the following locations aren't necessarily considered important pilgrimage sites in Buddhism, they reveal the devotion of the Buddha's disciples over centuries. What becomes evident as we look at these locations that span the Indian subcontinent is the spread of Buddhism over long distances and a number of cultures that have made this way of life their own. These are sites definitely worth visiting be it as a tourist or as a Buddhist practitioner.

The Ajanta Caves, India

Located in the state of modern-day Maharashtra in India, the Ajanta Caves contain paintings and also rock-cut sculptures that are considered masterpieces in Buddhist religious art.

Monks praying in Cave 26 at the Ajanta Caves

102

The construction work carried out these caves represent both the Theravada and Mahayana sects of Buddhism. A number of the paintings showcased in the Ajanta caves are derived from the Jataka Tales.

The Ellora Caves, India

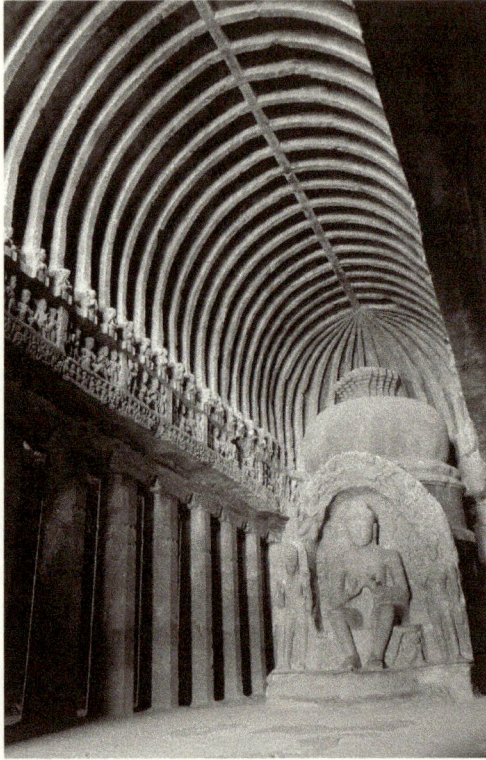

Carving of the Buddha at Carpenter's Cave – Ellora Caves

Quite clearly, the construction at these caves was funded by the royalty and was generally used by the monks as a place of rest during the rainy season. Merchants among other travelers also used this place to rest during the time it was constructed.

The Sanchi Stupa, India

Found in modern-day Madhya Pradesh, the Sanchi Stupa was built by Emperor Ashoka during his reign. As most Buddhists know, this stupa houses one of the relics of Buddha and has been expanded since the original monument was built.

The Sanchi Stupa from the Eastern Gate

Ornamental gateways, elaborate reliefs, sculptures are found at this stupa and is a site to visit if one wants to get a glimpse of Buddhist beliefs that have persisted over centuries. One should not forget the signature Ashoka pillars that are found at this site too.

The Jokhang Temple, Tibet

This Buddhist temple is located in Lhasa, the capital of Tibet and is widely considered to be the most important temple to Tibetans. Even if a certain Tibetan Buddhist sect currently maintains it, they allow all

Buddhists to visit this temple. This pilgrimage site, along with the Potala Palace and the Norbulingka, are visited not only by Tibetans but by Buddhists of all sects each year. Speaking of which the Potala Palace and Norbulingka were the residences of the Dalai Lama of Tibet until their government was dissolved in 1959 by China.

Jokhang Temple

Lake Manasarovar, Tibet

Located on the Tibetan Plateau, this lake is found near Mount Kailash and is also considered a sacred site for Buddhists. The Buddha is said to have visited this lake several times during his lifetime.

Yaks at Lake Mansarovar

In fact, most Tibetan Buddhists associate Lake Manasarovar with lake Anavatapta and is often the subject of several stories and teachings that are found in popular Buddhist literature. One can find the Chiu Monastery that is built on a steep hill in the region of this lake.

Anuradhapura, Sri Lanka

Anuradhapura, a city in Sri Lanka, is considered to be a center for Theravada Buddhism since it was home to several important Buddhist philosophers in its heyday. The Ruwanwelisaya Stupa is considered to be one of the tallest stupas standing at 103 feet.

The Ruwanwelisaya Stupa

Considered to be another sacred site to Buddhists from around the world, the stupa was in ruins by the 19th century. Thanks to the efforts of the Sinhalese bhikkhu, the stupa was restored by the year 1940.

Jaya Sri Maha Bodhi

This pipal tree is said to be grown from the southern branch of the Sri Maha Bodhi tree located in Bodh Gaya in India and is considered to be the oldest surviving tree. Planted in 288 BC, it is considered to be one of the most sacred relics by Buddhists both at home and abroad. Legend has it that the tree was brought King Ashoka's daughter where it was planted in the Mahamevnawa Gardens.

Boudhanath Temple, Nepal

Located in Kathmandu, Nepal, this stupa is considered to be one of the largest in Nepal and in the world. History records the fact that a number of Tibetan merchants have stayed at this location and prayed as it is an ancient trade route.

Jaya Sri Maha Bodhi

Even if the April 2015 earthquake in Nepal damaged the stupa, its reconstruction was completed with a central pole attached so as to replace the cracked spire.

Book 2: <u>Mind Hacking</u>

<u>Learn the Secrets to Change Your Mind to Positivity in 20 Days</u>

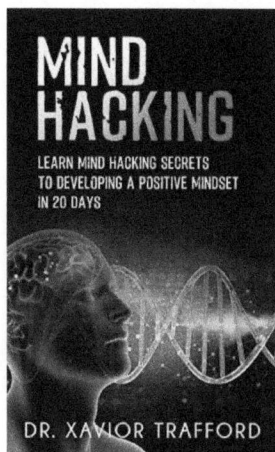

Positive Mindset for Success

Many thoughts arise in our heads and disappear. If you get a particularly original one, the first step to bring it to the real world is by writing it down. Then, it goes from being nothing to being something. Writing is like a bridge between our mind and our reality.

The first step is clarifying your ambitious thought. Once you have an idea what you want to achieve, write it down and pen down the biggest obstacle next to it.

Keeping a daily record leads to a higher chance of success.

The main reason why some people are truly successful in life is because they have managed to turn thoughts into actions. In order to achieve our ambitions, the first part of the whole process is thinking about how to do it effectively. In the upcoming chapters, we will discuss the action plan.

Benefits of writing down:

You don't have to commit to memory because more often than not, we forget things. We are forgetful creatures. Some of us even forget our own birthdays. So, you can't expect to remember a random thought. It is better to distance yourself from it too so that you can focus on other things effectively without worrying about it slipping from your mind.

- You have a clearer and fresher perspective on the idea then when it was only in your brain.

- When you first have the idea, you aren't completely aware of its details and feasibility. As time goes on, you can see if it's worth it or not.

- You can write down some of your own thoughts after going through the recommendations of other self-made successful people.

- The worst enemy of creative and innovative people is their own mind, as it constantly instills fear in them. When you carry on with something you are passionate about, you will start seeing the effectiveness of your efforts. At first, it will be hard, but you will then see improvement in your ideas too.

- Ideas are interesting and it's a thought-provoking conversation tactic.

- Ideas motivate people. You might get mocked for suggesting something crazy, but there is no genius without a little bit of madness.

Virtues of writing down a schedule everyday

Sometimes, after a particularly busy day, you tend to contemplate. You have managed to get a lot done during the day but when you think about it, you realize you didn't achieve anything truly valuable.

It is very important to schedule your time properly, and when you do so, you will slowly start to see an improvement in all aspects of your life, including your family, friends, work, and yourself. After thinking and working, a powernap also helps you regain focus.

Scheduling is planning ahead and dividing your task by priority into an appropriate time period. By doing so, you will have a much greater chance of achieving your goals in time. If you strictly follow your schedule, you will see the following benefits:

1. Giving important tasks enough time to get done.

2. If something unexpected comes up, which often happens, you have a contingency plan to deal with it efficiently without disrupting anything in your life.

3. You get to know the limit of what you can get done without burning yourself out.

4. Sometimes, life gets so complicated that your personal goals get left behind. With scheduling, you will find time to work on them as well.

5. Many people are under stress due to an imbalance in their work and family life. With scheduling, you can regain a balance

between both parts of your life.

Time is invaluable, and it's difficult to comprehend just how important it is. The following are ways to schedule your time.

1. First of all, identify how much time you have got on your hands.

2. Find out which actions are expected from you in your daily life. Make sure you have enough time to perform them effectively all while following your timetable.

3. Identify and prioritize the most important tasks. Put those activities in time slots where you know you will be most productive.

4. Don't forget to leave out some time for the compensation of tasks. You need these, because sometimes, unexpected things that you can't ignore pop up.

5. In your schedule, don't forget to include some time to edit and review the schedule itself.

6. While reviewing your activities, properly analyze whether they truly deserve your time or not. Try to carry out those activities in the most efficient way possible.

Habits of successful people:

The following are habits of highly successful people that might help you in your journey as well.

- People who are at the top of the ladder all had one thing in common. They recognized the value of time. Here are some of their habits that you can easily incorporate in your life to achieve your goals with a positive mindset.

- They avoided making useless decisions throughout the day. For example, you spend extra time and energy to pick out an outfit in the morning. Most successful people stick to a dress code. You should try to automate the tasks that require your precious mental energy.

- People who start early in the morning are more productive during the day. They also have a more positive outlook on their day because they have more time on their hands.

- Try to introduce frequent breaks to your daily work routine. If you think that working constantly from the beginning of the day until the end is how you will get maximum work done, you're wrong. Studies have found that after 52 minutes of work, a 17 minutes break will maximize your workout. (2019)28

- Try to spend your breaks outside rather than indoors. It will boost your creativity and productivity much more.

- Multitasking causes more harm than good. Don't fall into this trap.

- If you have a bunch of tasks lined up, you risk getting burned out. Prioritize yourself and your health first, and learn to say no whenever appropriate.

---

[28] (2019). Retrieved from https://lifehacker.com/52-minute-work-17-minute-break-is-the-ideal-productivi-1616541102

- Don't panic whenever things don't seem to go your way.

Complex Tasks

If you are suddenly faced with a massive, complex task, it is very easy to become overwhelmed and stressed. To tackle a big task, break it into manageable pieces.

Here are some ways to easily break down a complicated task:

- Make sure you understand the problem and its expected outcome. What is it supposed to look like after completion? Grasp the task fully.

- Try to separate parts of tasks. Make different steps and know which part should be done first, second, etc. Make an order that you are going to follow to complete the task.

- Set a deadline for each task. You will be more productive and focused if you give yourself a time period in which you will need to complete a task.

- Make sure that you stay on track. Remind yourself of the project in its entirety so that you don't lose focus.

- Always remember to set your timeline a little earlier than the actual final one.

- Work on the product thoroughly so that you can learn more about it and make it better with time.

- We always make plans for our life, but plans only work when you practically outline them to work out. You can't build a house by giving verbal instructions to constructors.

- It is best if you write down your goals. If you are able to vividly describe all your goals in written detail, you will have a higher chance of success. People who can distinctly describe their goals are 1.2 to 1.4 times more likely to achieve them than those who can't. ("Neuroscience Explains Why You Need to Write Down Your Goals If You Actually Want to Achieve Them", 2019)[29]. It seems like a tedious task, but it's definitely worth the trouble. Not many things make life more enjoyable than achieving your goals.

Writing is like creating something from nothing.

Writing things down has two levels:

1. External storage of an idea. You are not just storing it in your brain; you are physically saving it too. Put the paper you wrote it on in a place that you will see every day. Having a visual reminder every day helps you remember it much better.

2. Writing things down improves the encoding. Encoding is a process in which whatever we perceive goes to our brain's hippocampus. It is where the decision whether to store information in long-term memory or not happens. Writing improves this particular process.

3. When you write down goals, many cognitive processes are

---

[29] Neuroscience Explains Why You Need To Write Down Your Goals If You Actually Want To Achieve Them. (2019). Retrieved from https://www.forbes.com/sites/markmurphy/2018/04/15/neuroscience-explains-why-you-need-to-write-down-your-goals-if-you-actually-want-to-achieve-them/#3001926e7905

involved. First, you take a mental picture, then you transfer that thought from brain to paper. The generation effect is when people have a better memory of things they have produced themselves.

4. A study shows that people who take notes in the classroom remember more important facts.

5. Daily reminders can help create positive loops in your brain. Overrun old habits with new ones. Mask the old tracks with new ones in your life. Bad habits can ruin your life in many ways, so if you don't recognize and get rid of them, you are going to be stuck in the same place your whole life.

Neuroplasticity

Repeating thoughts and actions make up a new neural pathway. With each new small thought, we are able to subtly but surely change how our brains function. However, this only happens if we repeat it frequently.

Neuroplasticity is like muscles of the mind. If we train thoughts, they become strong, while those that we ignore fade away. As we age, the plasticity of our brain also decreases.

Stress and boredom are one of the main reasons why we develop bad habits. You can also adopt them from your household or from the company you keep. We will particularly focus on ones caused by stress and boredom.

To truly identify the causes of your bad habits, you have to be honest with yourself.

Every habit has two different sides. For example, going on social media as soon as you wake up and frequently throughout the day helps you feel connected but it also reduces your productivity. So, bad habits are a bit complex to break out of because of the small rewards they offer.

When you think about your bad habits, they benefit you in a way, that is why it is so hard to break out of them. That is why you can't simply cut them out; you need to replace them. The replacement habit has to also provide some kind of similar benefit. Here are some methods to employ to get rid of bad habits in your life.

- Find a replacement for it. When the urge to commit a bad habit appears in your mind, you need to plan what you are going to do ahead of time. Whatever you are dealing with, make a plan for it and carry that out instead of falling back to your old habit.

- Remove triggers that may prompt you to carry out one of your bad habits. Make it easier on yourself to cut bad habits in your life by avoiding elements and events that cause them in the first place.

- The company that you keep is important. Your friends and surroundings matter. It is important to surround yourself with positive people who could actually help you in feeling good and positive about yourself and your life so surround yourself with the right kind of people.

- You can visualize the successful feeling and how amazing it will be to finally not have gotten rid of a certain bad habit in your life. It will further motivate you to ignore the need that compels you to revert to your old habit.

- It helps greatly if you know someone struggling with the same thing, as you can motivate each other and it is nice to know you are not fighting this battle alone. Someone is also doing it, and if they can do, it so can I.

- You will not transform into a new person by letting go of your bad habits. It will simply make you a better version of yourself.

- We all make mistakes, but the key is learning from them. So, don't give up by making a mistake. Learn and move on from it by being the wiser version of yourself.

Repetition is key

Our mind also makes neural tracks of the habits we repeat. So, with repetition, we can make new pathways. Our mind cannot be controlled, only trained with effort and persistence.

A way to have a positive outlook is to often remind yourself of positivity. You can also keep a tracking app etc.

In order to achieve a personal goal, you have to remember it and keep it in your mind most of the time. If you don't think about it enough, it will be nearly impossible to achieve it. Here are some tips to add reminders of goals in your life.

Keep reminders in every environment you are part of in your daily routine, like your office or your room. You should be able to see them every day.

Piia Rauha

We should also recite our goals to ourselves when we have little or nothing on our mind, such as driving to work, taking a walk, eating etc. If we are serious about it, we should reminiscence about our goals whenever we can. Silently recite whatever you want to achieve.

What is a Mental Simulation?

A simulation means playing out a process before finalizing it. So, a mental simulation means doing the same with our thoughts and ideas. Before we act on something, we go through it in our brain to come up with a probable conclusion.

Mental simulation is a very powerful tool that we have at our disposal, and we make us of it very often. We quickly guess if something is a good thing or not. Our brains always try to predict the future based on what is happening around us. As a result of actions, we undertake our brain's guesses about what is going to happen as a result. This is a very big advantage. When we are faced with atypical problems, this technique helps us to solve them.

Mental simulation is how mankind has learned to escape various life-threatening situations. If we are faced with a situation that we have never been in before, we can use mental association to assess whether it is dangerous for us or not. For example, jumping in a swamp that could possibly be inhabited by crocodiles. We can use an association in this mental situation to reach a result. We will associate what we know about crocodiles and how they hide before an attack to reach the conclusion that it is probably not a good idea to jump in.

Our mental simulation is dependent on our memory and how we perceive things. It also relies on the memory of the experiences we have faced in our lives. Mental simulation is like a laboratory where any experiment or scenario could be played without any conscious thought. You can test the most ridiculous of ideas without any risk. You can also imagine a goal and from where you stand, you can develop a full-fledged roadmap to your goal. To actually reap these benefits, you have to train this ability.

To hone our mental abilities means to learn and challenge ourselves. With learning new things comes changes. The changes help increase our brain's health by increasing our memory reserves. The following are some of the main components of mental exercise that help improve our mental simulation:

We should always challenge our abilities. We shouldn't fall into boring and routine patterns.

Always thinking up new and creative things is also very good for the brain. The most important parts of our brain, such as the prefrontal cortex benefit from taking on new cognitive challenges.

It is better to stimulate different areas of our brain and engage in activities that make use of different functions of our brains, rather than sticking to one type of task.

Benefits of mental simulation

1. You will be better equipped to handle any setbacks because when you mentally anticipate a scenario in your head, you anticipate the potential setbacks.

2. You will have more faith in yourself. Actually, playing out multiple scenarios in your head makes you feel more confident about your ideas, and you won't be scared to chase them in real life. In reality, pursuing a goal in real life can seem

intimidating, especially if you are flying blind.

3. When you set a goal or destination in your head to try mental simulation, you will come up with various plans in order to reach them. When you come up with several plans, it will help you know which is best.

4. There is a difference between visualization and simulation of our goals. You are not only able to think about positives but also work on negative things as well.

Try a hybrid approach of both mental simulations and write down your goals meticulously.

Collaboration

If you want to build more trusting relationships and have a more effective work environment, radical collaboration is necessary. To reap radical collaboration's many benefits, you must first have an intent to collaborate.

To do a collaboration, you require:

- A skill-set

- A mindset.

Radical collaboration has the following advantages:

- It increases a sense of community, builds teamwork, and builds trust with the right people.

- Sharing your ideas and thoughts with other people makes you more effective in your own work.

- You can get out of the harmful defensive mindset. It costs you valuable mind energy which you would much rather spend on more constructive thoughts. Defensive behavior is not attractive and it could be your downfall. You can develop an early warning system to resist the defensive behavior that threatens to surface. Develop an action plan that you can implement whenever you feel like you are being defensive again.

- It increases problem-solving. Two heads are always better than one.

Radical collaboration teaches five essential skills which are:

1. It will conjure an atmosphere of truthfulness which is much more productive and healthier for our mind.

2. You learn self-accountability. You know you have to deliver equally as much as the other person. You become aware of the responsibility that you have to fulfill. You are not only aware of your own needs but also feel a responsibility for the sake of the other party.

3. One of the most empowering thoughts to have when you are down is that you have the power to change your beliefs. You can create a much better life if you renew the way you think and make it more open and creative. This way, you will have more choices available to you than ever before and will start taking accountability for your future actions.

4. Negotiating through tough cycles in a relationship is a very good skill that you can polish through radical collaboration. Going back and forth between two point-of-views helps as you

consider the other's viewpoint as well. Don't think that negotiating will come easy even if you are one of the most self-aware, honest, non- defensive people you know.

5. According to an old saying, you cannot expect to solve problems with the same mind that created it. When we get stuck on a code, we tend to seek help from another fellow. They might have a different mindset and will be able to find the problem much quicker than you. More great ideas are brought to life thanks to the collaboration of different types of minds.

Book 3: <u>Mindfulness</u>

<u>How to Maximize Mind Power, Boost Mindfulness Through Transcendental Meditation and Maintain A Healthy, Spiritually-Awakened Life</u>

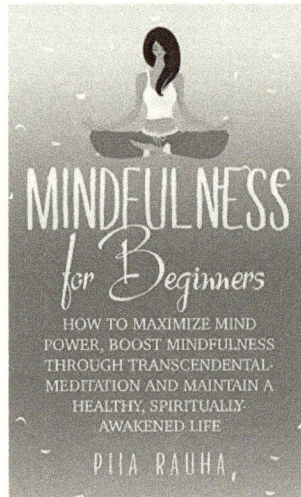

Why We Feel Stress

Stress is a natural phenomenon caused by the body in response to events that are perceived as harmful or threatening. This perception of danger is not always conscious. For example, when you suddenly see a tiger across the road, your body's defense system is automatically activated, releasing large amounts of stress hormones, cortisol and adrenaline, into your bloodstream. Your heart rate and blood pressure get spiked, muscles become tense, breathing gets faster and your senses elevate. All of this is an involuntary response called "Fight or Flight", where your body prepares you to either fight the threat (in this case, a tiger) or run away from it.

As you can guess, not all stress is bad. In fact, if it weren't for stress, we wouldn't be alive. This is not to say that all kinds of stress are positive. When stress occurs in an unguided manner and in heavy doses, it can lead to a lot of health issues (both physical and mental).

How to Eliminate Stress with Mindfulness

There is a difference between response and reaction. The difference is that a response is generated after thinking and processing the stimulus whereas a reaction is impulsive. Mindfulness can help you become more responsive instead of reactive.

People who experience and understand stress will know that everyone has unique stress triggers and stress reactions. The stress triggers occur when the subject feels harm or threat to their survival at a subliminal level. To relieve this stress and deflate the threat, a stress response is generated. And the stress response varies among individuals: for some, it is eating junk food or drugs or gambling while for others it is exercise or spending time with their family or pets. A healthy stress response will build your personality and make you stronger.

What mindfulness does is build a gap between the stress trigger and stress response. This gives you more time to analyze the situation, cool down and choose the right response. Instead of doing the bad things in a haste, you will be more inclined to normalize the stress by looking at the situation objectively.

It has also been found that practicing mindfulness will reduce neural activity in a part of your brain called the amygdala. It is responsible for identifying threats in the environment and hijack our cortex (responsible for critical thinking) if there is any possibility of danger. Sadly, the hypersensitivity of amygdala results in too many stress triggers and immediate stress responses. So, mindfulness can actually help you turn the amygdala's intervention down a notch and experience less stress.

Mindfulness Trick for Handling Stress

What you want to do is remember and imagine vividly the situation that triggered your stress. Since stress is a psychological phenomenon, you can pay attention to the various body parts, sensations and feelings that are changing because of the stress. Pay close attention and try to spot the emotion that is responsible for the stress precisely. Be mindful of the emotion and what it does to your body. Try to feel the changes in your body in conjunction with breathing and relaxation. If you can, put your hand on the location of your body which feels affected and gently massage it with a sense of compassion and care. With enough practice, you should be able to not only handle stress but avoid it altogether by developing stress resistance.

Modern Day Mindfulness

Before we study more modern aspects, let us first get a perspective of the origin of mindfulness and its history.

We can trace back the practice of mindfulness to at least a couple-of-thousand years ago. Many spiritual practices have used mindfulness as a gateway to reach the inner self. Arguably, Buddhism has been the most influential religion in regards to developing mental practices for streamlining the consciousness. Founded in the sixth century BCE, it has adopted mindfulness as one of its core values. In fact, Gautama

Buddha, the Indian prince who started Buddhism, has included mindfulness as one of the eight folds of the noble path to reach nirvana or enlightenment. The ancient Indian practice of Hatha Yoga (a form of yoga that relies on physical postures for development of body and mind) has also inspired many aspects of the present-day mindfulness techniques.

Buddhism experienced vast success and expansion in India when Ashoka of the Mauryan Empire converted to Buddhism after the battle of Kalinga, one of India's biggest and bloodiest battles. After the battle was won, apparently Ashoka the emperor realized the amount of destruction he had caused and chose to follow the path of non-violence or ahimsa. Forty years of peace and prosperity followed after that choice. During this period, many convoys were sent throughout Asia to enlighten people of the importance of mindfulness and Buddhist practices to elevate the consciousness. However, with the Muslim invasion of India and the anti-Buddhist political situation in Southeast Asian countries like Tibet and Vietnam, Buddhism had experienced a relative low in the early twentieth century.

Many Buddhist monks and spiritual teachers migrated to the west and reconfigured the Buddhist practices to fit the western lifestyle. Out of this came the more contemporary techniques of mindfulness and meditation that we see today. Many people like Jon Kabat Zinn, Thich Nhat Hanh and Shunryu Suzuki were influential in propagating mindfulness in the west. A relatively popular name we often hear of is Dalai Lama, the spiritual leader of Tibet.

In the twenty-first century, we have seen people like Tara Brach and Eckhart Tolle spread the message of mindfulness and its important role in daily well-being. The mindfulness techniques taught today are mostly secular and scientific. So, you are not obligated to follow Buddhism or any other religion to reap the benefits of mindfulness. Many programs and retreats are accessible to the general public today. One famous program is called MBSR, which has spread like wildfire in the west and is responsible for helping thousands of people deal better with their pain and a wide range of psychological issues. Let's look into that now.

MBSR – Mindfulness-Based Stress Reduction

MBSR is a clinical treatment that involves a lot of mindfulness meditation and body awareness to reduce mental and physical disorders. In more recent years, MBSR has been prevalent as a treatment for stress reduction, relaxation and anxiety control. As we've discussed in the previous section, this program has its roots in the eastern practices of Buddhism and Hatha Yoga, but present-day MBSR is mostly secular. In fact, it has become a standardized health care technique to improve quality of life using mindfulness.

Breathing Exercises for Mindfulness

So, why exactly should one indulge in mindful breathing in the very first instance?

The thing is, mindfulness breathing can help us become more aware of what we are thinking and feeling, in a completely non-judgmental way. There is a vast plethora of research that has shown us exactly how mindfulness is linked to improved health, decreased anxiety and even a stronger resilience towards stress.

The way it works is really simple: mindfulness breathing can offer us that vital 'anchor' – that is our breath – on which we can focus whenever we feel we are struggling with those negative thoughts. It can also assist us in being 'present' in the here and now.

So, ready to take a look at some stellar breathing exercises for mindfulness? Let's go!

Some succinct breathing exercises for mindfulness:

The Simple Mindful Breathing Exercise

This one is really the simplest mindful breathing exercise there is. Let's take a look at how it works.

Step One – Get comfortable. To make the most of this breathing exercise, you have to be as comfortable as you can possibly be. So, ensure you find a quiet place and then sit down on a cushion or chair or perhaps even lie down on your back. Ensure that your arms and hands relax comfortably.

Step Two – Gradually become aware. Now is the time to become fully aware of your surroundings. This is the time you wish to bring your attention to the 'present', by observing the sensations in your body. You want to run a check of your body from head to toe and consciously release any tension that might be there.

Step Three – Become aware of your breath. Now is the time to focus on your breath. You have to notice the sensation of your breath going in and out. There is no need to modulate your breathing in any which way. As you breathe, make sure you are aware of the rise and the fall of your chest and abdomen. Here is where you wish to pay attention to the sensations of your breath, one at a time. You need to follow the breath right through its full duration.

Step Four – Do not worry if the mind wanders. Through the course of your focus on your breath, you will find that your mind is prone to wander. Do not let this affect you in any which way. When thoughts arise, do not simply keep flitting from one thought to another. Observe the thought in your mind, accept it and then return your focus to your breathing. Simply accept the thoughts that arise and then return your focus back to breathing.

Step Five – Continue this practice of mindful breathing for five to ten minutes from the time you start. You want that breathing exercise of yours to last at least five minutes; hence it is prudent that you set a timer to the requisite amount so that you know exactly when it is over without having to constantly refer to your watch to see exactly how much time has elapsed. As discussed in the point above, you might occasionally find yourself getting lost in that train of thought, but that doesn't matter – all you need to do is come back to your breathing.

Scan your body before you checkout. Before you do, however, you need to once again take note of your entire body and the way you are feeling. Ensure that you have a sense of immense gratitude for immersing yourself in a practice that has worked wonders for your well-being.

Now that you have seen this lovely and beautifully simple technique of breathing that will help you get rooted in mindfulness, let's take a look at yet another breathing exercise that can work wonders for you!

Another Variation of Mindful Breathing

The more the merrier, right? Here's another breathing exercise you can effectively employ for your well-being.

Piia Rauha

Step One – Get comfortable again. As discussed in the previous breathing technique, you really wish to be as comfortable as you can be. Then, you are ready to get into the breathing practice.

Step Two – Focus on your breath (while counting to three), then hold your breath (count to two), followed by a long exhale through your mouth (count to four).

Step Three – Continue this process. Continue this very same process while at the very same time just being aware of every single breath without regulating it, while you are using the chest and the sensation of your breath through your nostrils.

Step Four – Don't mind those thoughts. As touched upon in the earlier breathing exercise, you do not wish to give any sort of attention to those thoughts that come your way while you are indulging in your breathing practice. As before, ensure that you merely observe those thoughts and then let them go.

References

Baer, D. (2016, December 12). A Psychiatrist on Why Your Mind 'Has a Mind of Its Own? Retrieved from https://www.thecut.com/2016/12/a-psychiatrist-on-why-your-mind-has-a-mind-of-its-own.html

Cameron, Y. (2019, September 10). A Beginner's Guide To The 7 Chakras. Retrieved from https://www.mindbodygreen.com/0-91/The-7-Chakras-for-Beginners.html

Die Before You Die. (2016, July 28). Retrieved from http://montywinters.com/awareness/die-before-you-die/

Feelings and Emotions: The A - Z Guide. (2019, August 7). Retrieved from https://www.laughteronlineuniversity.com/feelings-and-emotions/

Finding Your Inner Compass: The Most Powerful Guidance You'll Ever Need is Right There in Your Heart. (2019, February 28). Retrieved from https://katiedejong.com/finding-your-inner-compass/

The Four Noble Truths. (n.d.). Retrieved from https://www.bbc.co.uk/religion/religions/buddhism/beliefs/fournobletruths_1.shtml

How Negative is Your "Mental Chatter"? (n.d.). Retrieved from https://www.psychologytoday.com/us/blog/sapient-nature/201310/how-negative-is-your-mental-chatter

How To Open Your Third Eye: Awaken Your Spirituality. (2016, March 11). Retrieved from https://www.psychics4today.com/how-to-open-your-third-eye-chakra/

If You Meet the Buddha on the Road, Kill Him. (n.d.). Retrieved from https://fractalenlightenment.com/26323/spirituality/if-you-meet-the-buddha-on-the-road-kill-him

The Long Journey to the Inner Self. (2014, August 23). Retrieved from https://www.huffpost.com/entry/the-long-journey-to-the-inner-self_b_5518540

Pain Body - What It Is and How To Be Free — InnerPeaceNow.com. (2016, September 2). Retrieved from https://www.innerpeacenow.com/inner-peace-blog/pain-body

Spiritual Awakening is not the Same as Enlightenment. (2014, September 28). Retrieved from https://www.heartki.com/spiritual-awakening-enlightenment/

Spiritual Awakening Signs: 10 Authentic Symptoms + 5 Spiritual Traps. (2019, August 30). Retrieved from https://scottjeffrey.com/spiritual-awakening-signs/

Spiritual Awakening Signs: 10 Authentic Symptoms + 5 Spiritual Traps. (2019, August 30). Retrieved from https://scottjeffrey.com/spiritual-awakening-signs/

Third Eye Awakening Explained - Inner Outer Peace. (2019, April 2). Retrieved from https://innerouterpeace.com/third-eye-awakening/

Third Eye Guide – What is the Third Eye? (2019, September 12). Retrieved from https://personaltao.com/third-eye/

The True Meaning of Living in the Present Moment. (2018, June 13). Retrieved from https://www.pocketmindfulness.com/live-in-the-present-moment/

What is a Kundalini Awakening? (2017, March 6). Retrieved from https://foreverconscious.com/what-is-a-kundalini-awakening

"What Is Spiritual Enlightenment - Enlightenment Podcast." http://www.enlightenmentpodcast.com/spiritual-enlightenment-spiritual-awakening/. Accessed 17 Sep. 2019.

What is a Kundalini Awakening? (2017, March 6). Retrieved from https://foreverconscious.com/what-is-a-kundalini-awakening

What is Chi? (2019, August 25). Retrieved from https://www.energyarts.com/what-is-chi/

What Is Spiritual Enlightenment | Dr. Puff. (n.d.). Retrieved from http://www.enlightenmentpodcast.com/spiritual-enlightenment-spiritual-awakening/

What's The Difference Between Feelings And Emotions? (2019, April 23). Retrieved from https://www.thebestbrainpossible.com/whats-the-difference-between-feelings-and-emotions/

www.ingramcontent.com/pod-product-compliance
Lightning Source LLC
Chambersburg PA
CBHW030841090426
42737CB00009B/1056